TRAVEL ARIZONA
The Back Roads

TWENTY BACK ROAD TOURS FOR THE WHOLE FAMILY

ARIZONA
HIGHWAYS BOOK

Text by James E. Cook, Sam Negri, Marshall Trimble
Edited by Dean Smith
Cartography by Don Bufkin
Color Photography by Arizona Highways Contributors
Design & Production by W. Randall & Deirdre A. Irvine
Book Editor — Wesley Holden

Contents

Travel Arizona: The Back Roads

Prepared by the Book Division of *Arizona Highways* magazine, a monthly publication of the Arizona Department of Transportation.

Nina M. La France — Publisher / Bob Albano — Managing Editor / Robert J. Farrell — Associate Editor / Cindy Mackey — Production Director / Vicky Snow and Ellen Straine — Production Assistants

Copyright © 1989 by Arizona Department of Transportation, State of Arizona. Fifth Printing, 1997. All rights reserved. Printed in Japan. No part of this book may be reproduced in any form or means without permission from *Arizona Highways*, 2039 West Lewis Avenue, Phoenix, AZ 85009.

Library of Congress Catalog Number 88-71756   ISBN 0-916179-54-0

(ABOVE) *Tour 11 leads through some dramatic back country, from the desert near Roosevelt Lake, to the pines atop the Sierra Ancha Mountains.* WESLEY HOLDEN

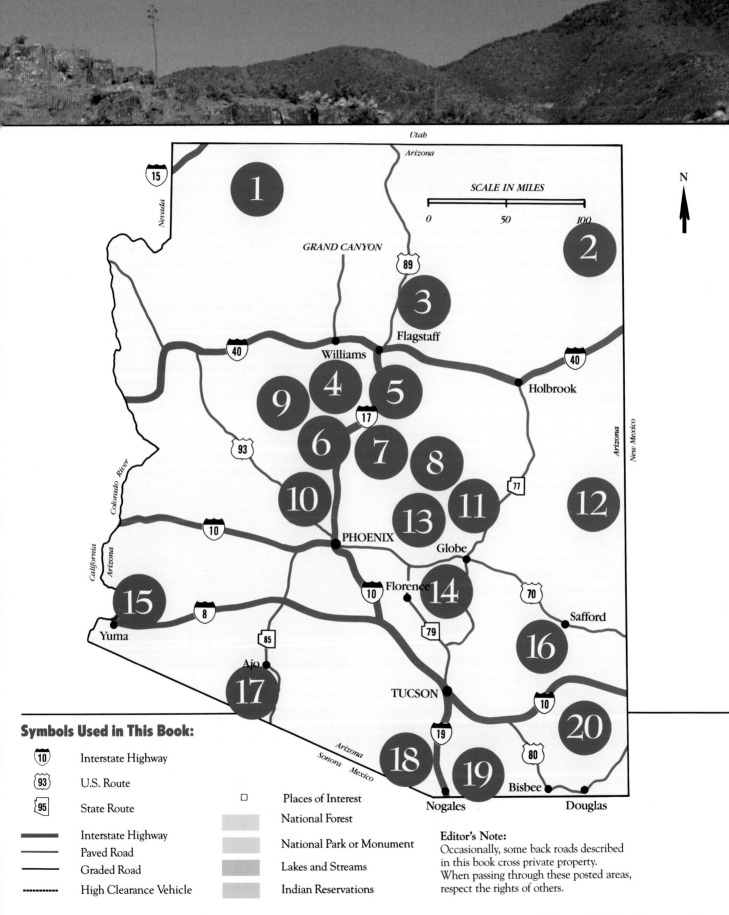

Symbols Used in This Book:

10	Interstate Highway
93	U.S. Route
95	State Route
——	Interstate Highway
——	Paved Road
——	Graded Road
----------	High Clearance Vehicle

□	Places of Interest
	National Forest
	National Park or Monument
	Lakes and Streams
	Indian Reservations

Editor's Note:
Occasionally, some back roads described in this book cross private property. When passing through these posted areas, respect the rights of others.

Introduction

When a travel book is received with such overwhelming approval as was *Travel Arizona*, published in 1983 by *Arizona Highways* and reprinted seven times, it most certainly deserves a sequel. Those who have enjoyed the 16 paved-highway tours described in that book now will be eager to take the next step: venturing onto the back roads to experience a side of Arizona which less adventuresome folks will never see.

Travel Arizona: The Back Roads continues the tradition of helping people "discover" the beauty of the land, not to conquer it, but to be at peace with it. Travel these back roads and you will be introduced to quiet places where you can listen to the birds, smell the flowers, touch the earth, watch the sunset, and learn something of Arizona's heritage. You can venture top-to-bottom and border-to-border of this magnificent state, from awesome Toroweap and the Arizona Strip Country in the far north to a charming sojourn along the Mexican border from Nogales to Coronado National Memorial. These 20 tours offer enjoyment for the whole family.

You will thrill to the same breathtaking view from the Mogollon Rim that captivated Army wife Martha Summerhayes when she traveled Crook's Trail in 1874. You will marvel at the variety of birds along the Colorado River near Yuma, the desert grandeur of Organ Pipe Cactus National Monument, and the green-clad mountains of remote Blue River Country.

Most of these are circle tours that can be completed in one unhurried day, and in the family automobile. (High-clearance or four-wheel drive vehicles are suggested where roads are more challenging.) In each tour, mileages and routes are carefully indicated, as is the degree of difficulty for each journey.

Our guides on these adventures are three seasoned veterans of Arizona backcountry exploring. Marshall Trimble is a popular historian, teacher, and cowboy balladeer. Jim Cook for years wrote a fascinating column on Arizona history in *The Arizona Republic*. Sam Negri is a widely read southern Arizona writer and a prolific contributor to *Arizona Highways* magazine.

The late Don Bufkin of Tucson was one of Arizona's most respected mapmakers. His detailed maps will guide

you along the highways and byways of each tour.

Having written many articles and edited an earlier book for *Arizona Highways*, I was excited to join Marsh, Jim, Sam, and Don, and to serve as editor of the book.

Be forewarned: Most of these tours are not Sunday drives over paved highways. Restaurants and service stations will be encountered only infrequently, so you should start each trip with all the food and gasoline you will need. You'll find campgrounds on many of these tours, as well as fishing, boating, and hiking trails. So come prepared to enjoy all the opportunities.

Arizona's back road wonderland is still unspoiled, so be sure to leave it that way. Pick up any litter you might find there and bring it out with you. For everyone's sake, both today and tomorrow, resolve to leave this land better than you found it.

You'll discover to your delight that many of Arizona's most scenic wonders and historic treasures are off the well-traveled highways. White Horse Lake, Sycamore Canyon, Apache Trail, Rustler Park, Swift Trail, ghost towns, Indian cliff dwellings and historic cavalry posts — all these and many more adventures await you on Arizona's byways.

Take your camera, your fishing gear, your bird books, and especially your sense of adventure. You really haven't seen how amazing Arizona is until you've ventured onto its delightful back roads.

— Dean Smith

(TOP) *Bright summer flowers and emerald mountains beckon on the scenic road to Blue in eastern Arizona's wilderness, south of Alpine.* PETER ENSENBERGER

Arizona Strip Country

Fredonia • Pipe Spring National Monument • Spectacular Toroweap
Mount Trumbull • Main Street Valley • Hurricane Cliffs • St. George

White line cowboys and dirt road addicts alike will love this adventure into some of America's most remote country. Toroweap, at the edge of the Grand Canyon, is the highlight, and nothing you've seen before can prepare you for this awesome view.

This is a demanding trip, including nearly 160 miles of dirt road, some of which call for a high-clearance vehicle, but it's an experience you won't forget. The loop drive starts at Fredonia near the Utah border, 197 miles north of Flagstaff, goes to Toroweap and Mt. Trumbull, and returns to Fredonia via Colorado City, Arizona, or St. George, Utah.

This is the Arizona Strip — 11,000 square miles of melancholy empty space that is home to a little more than 3,000 residents. It's also a land of beautifully sculptured mesas and painted plains, bounded largely on the north by the variegated Vermilion Cliffs and on the south by the Grand Canyon. Historically, the Strip has been separated, culturally and geographically, from the rest of Arizona.

So isolated is this land that the people of the now-deserted village of Mount Trumbull had to travel 278 miles through three states just to reach their county seat at Kingman. Mormons began settling this area in the 1860s, and most people here today trace their roots to those early colonists.

The Kaibab Plateau is a huge "island" that rises nearly 4,000 feet above the surrounding mile-high Strip country. This plateau is high and wet, but the rest of the Strip is so dry that people say the bushes follow

Best time to go
April through November

Degree of difficulty
Moderate to demanding

Type of vehicle
High clearance preferred

Travel time
12 hours minimum; suggest overnight camping at Toroweap

Road type
Dirt, sometimes rough; impassable in rain

Elevation
5,000 - 8,000 feet

Terrain
High desert

Features
Exceptional Grand Canyon view, history

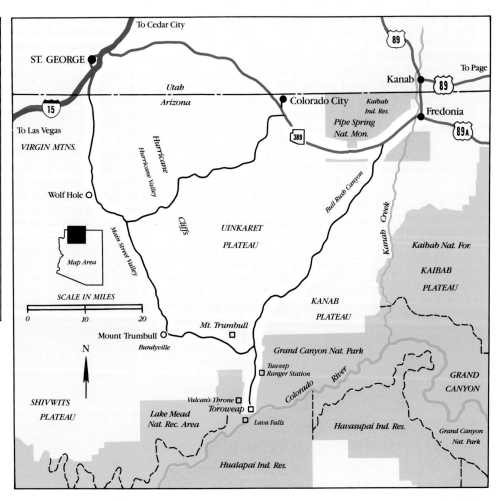

(LEFT) *The Arizona Strip is a wild, lonesome land. This road takes you to spectacular Toroweap Overlook on the North Rim of Grand Canyon.*
DAVID ELMS

dogs around, and cows give powdered milk.

Fill up your gas tank and load up on water and food in Fredonia, because it's a long way around and back.

You may want to start with a visit to historic Pipe Spring National Monument, 15 miles west of Fredonia on paved State Route 389. It was a launching pad for Mormon settlement during the 1870s. A fort was built there in 1870, and Arizona's first telegraph station was established there in 1871.

Our back road journey begins nine miles west of Fredonia on State Route 389. Turn south off that paved highway to a well-traveled dirt road that goes 58 miles to Toroweap. The road runs east of Bull Rush Canyon across the high desert. It's quiet out here — only the lonesome wail of the wind breaks the silence.

The Tuweep Ranger Station is picturesquely nestled against a salmon-colored butte about a mile inside Grand Canyon National Park. It's another six miles to the primitive campground at the rim of the Canyon. At this point the road becomes fairly rough, punctuated by sandstone outcroppings.

And then you're at Toroweap.

First impressions are as varied as the backgrounds of the visitors. The visitors register contains some of their written comments: "Incredible"… "Spiritual"… "Held onto my kids and later had nightmares, but I loved it!"

My approach was typical. First I walked boldly up to the edge, peered over, and then quickly retreated. I removed my hat and put a rock on it, lest the wind carry it into the chasm far below. Then I cautiously crawled up to the edge on all fours for another look. Large sandstone boulders provide natural thrones to sit on and reflect on this awesome place. The only sound is the wind rushing through the canyon and the distant roar of Lava Falls, some 3,000 feet below.

(ABOVE) *You may have difficulty finding words to describe Toroweap, but you can record your comments in the visitors register.* DAVID ELMS

(RIGHT) *An awestruck visitor to Toroweap Overlook peers into the Grand Canyon, nearly 3,000 feet straight down.* RANDY PRENTICE

I camped overnight, and next morning found a rocky crag where I could hang on and lean over the edge to see Vulcan's Throne, a lava neck poking out of the middle of the Colorado River. Raftsmen consider it good luck, I'm told, to touch it with their craft before going over the 30-foot drop at Lava Falls.

As Lady Luck would have it, I met a group of Sierra Club hikers and walked with them along the rocky edge of Saddle Horse Canyon to a spring, where we paused for a cool drink. Then it was time for us to resume the journey.

Leaving Toroweap, our route takes us back up the road from the campground, 13 miles to the junction that leads to Mt. Trumbull and Nixon Spring. It's seven miles on a gradual climb back through the piñon-juniper zone into the tall ponderosa pine country. From Nixon Spring, it's 2.7 miles on a winding side road to the summit of Mt. Trumbull. The Mormon pioneers cut timber on this mountain from 1871 to 1876 and hauled it 80 miles on wagons over the Temple Trail to St. George, Utah, to build the temple there.

We'll follow the old trail near the Hurricane Cliffs. Mule deer have been here as long as anyone can remember, but the pronghorn (antelope) and wild turkeys are transplants. There are elk and bighorn sheep, too.

The descent off the Uinkaret Plateau takes us to Main Street Valley and the gaunt remains of Mount Trumbull, a ghost town still referred to locally as "Bundyville" after the family who pioneered the town in 1916. The only building left on Main Street is the schoolhouse. Across the valley, a scattering of abandoned dwellings can be seen. Sagebrush now covers the land that was once ranched and farmed before drought chased the dreamers away.

I sat in the middle of the deserted town, watching a dust devil collide with the schoolhouse. The voice on the radio in my pickup gave the five o'clock traffic report in Phoenix . . . I was glad I was here.

Now we begin the return portion of our loop, traveling north from Mount Trumbull on Main Street, which becomes a well-maintained gravel road. After 21 miles we reach a junction. For those who want to drive on to civilization at St. George, Utah, take the left fork and travel 43 miles on dirt road. Fredonia is 81 miles east of St. George on a paved highway.

But the scenic route back to Fredonia turns right at the junction and heads for Colorado City. The road is narrow for the first few miles as you climb out of Main Street Valley and drop into Hurricane Valley. To the east are the limestone-colored cliffs that extend as far as you can see each way. Near the base of the cliffs are markers for the Temple Trail. Here, more than a century after they were made, wagon ruts are still visible on the trail to St. George.

Climbing onto the Uinkaret Plateau, you're treated to a spectacular view of the red sandstone mountains, part of the Vermilion Cliffs, that mantle the Arizona Strip. Nestled picturesquely at the foot of these mountains is the isolated community of Colorado City.

It's 35 miles on from Colorado City to our journey's end at Fredonia. You've traveled a long way, but you'll always be glad you came.

— *Marshall Trimble*

(ABOVE) *Leaving Toroweap, we move westward past Mt. Trumbull to Main Street Valley and the Temple Trail, over which Mormon pioneers hauled timber for the temple at St. George, Utah* (INSET RIGHT), *more than a century ago.* (INSET LEFT) *Lonely Mt. Trumbull towers in the background, above a rain-drenched road. When wet, this road can become a stern test, even for four-wheel drive vehicles.* PHOTOS BY RICHARD EMBERY

(BOTTOM) *The fort at historic Pipe Spring National Monument, 15 miles west of Fredonia, was a launching pad for Mormon settlement of Arizona Territory in the 1870s.* DAVID ELMS

Navajo Canyonlands

Hubbell Trading Post • Canyon de Chelly
Cliff dwellings and scenic overlooks • Fort Defiance • Window Rock

For a close-up look at Arizona's Navajo culture and the spectacular scenery of the Navajo canyonlands, this tour is hard to beat. Plan to spend at least two days to enjoy it properly.

The trek begins at the historic Hubbell Trading Post at Ganado, on U.S. Route 191, 39 miles north of the Chambers exit off Interstate 40 in northeastern Arizona. Your first view of the venerable red stone Hubbell post will provide you a cherished memory on the Arizona back roads. For more than a century, this fascinating post has been a social and commercial oasis on the lonesome high desert of the Colorado Plateau.

This is much more than a general store. It's a huge stone and adobe hacienda complete with barns, corrals, warehouses, and residence. The rustic interior has changed little since those bygone days when the legendary Don Juan Lorenzo Hubbell and his Navajo friends sat in the "bull pen" on a cold winter's day and visited around the red-hot cast iron stove.

Hubbell was born in New Mexico in 1854 and as a young man came to Arizona and lived with the Hopis and Navajos. In 1876 his Navajo friend Ganado Mucho (Many Cattle) took Hubbell to this site and convinced him that he should open a trading post here. Hubbell named the place in honor of his friend. Today the post belongs to the National Park Service and has been designated a National Historic Site.

Our next important stop through *Dinetah*

(ABOVE) *This bleached skull and sign mark the historic Hubbell Trading Post at Ganado, which has served the Navajo people for more than a century.* KEN AKERS

(LEFT) *Spider Rock, an 800-foot-high monolith in Canyon de Chelly, is the legendary home of Spider Woman. Navajo mothers warn their children to be good, or Spider Woman will eat them.* WILLARD CLAY

(Navajoland) is Canyon de Chelly National Monument. Follow State Route 264 five miles west and then turn north on U.S. Route 191, 30 miles to Chinle. Chinle is Navajo for "the place where it flows from the canyon." The town is well-named, for it sits just beyond the junction of Canyon del Muerto and Canyon de Chelly, the two major scenic features of the national monument.

Best time to go	April through October
Degree of difficulty	Easy
Type of vehicle	Family car
Travel time	Two days; overnight at Chinle or camp at Canyon de Chelly
Road type	Paved
Elevation	5,000 - 7,000 feet
Terrain	High desert, canyons
Features	Navajo culture, scenery

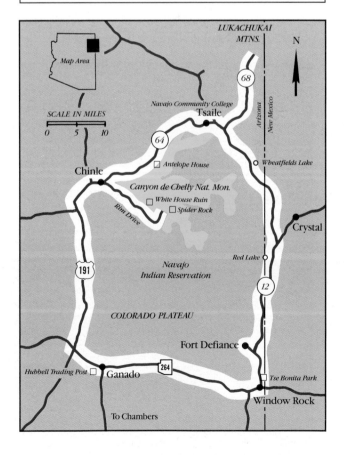

Canyon del Muerto (Canyon of the Dead) was the site of a massacre of Navajos by Spanish troops in 1805. Lieutenant Antonio Narbona's soldiers fired their muskets into a cave, and the ricocheting bullets killed 115 huddled Navajos.

"De Chelly" (pronounced deh-SHAY) is a name of several possible derivations — Spanish, Navajo, or English — and probably means "among the cliffs" or "rock canyon."

From the air, the two canyons resemble a huge turkey track. They are awe-inspiring, both from the air and peering over the steep precipice to the floor at a depth of nearly a thousand feet in places.

But to capture the essence of this wonderland, you must go down into the canyons. Tourists aren't allowed in the canyons without a park ranger or authorized guide, except on the trail into White House Ruin. All-day or half-day truck tours are available year-around. Stop at the visitor center for information. Overnight accommodations at local lodges must be reserved well in advance. (Remember that the Navajo Nation observes daylight saving time while the rest of Arizona does not.) Nearby National Park Service Cottonwood campground has 95 campsites.

Be sure to take the two-hour Rim Drive along the south side of Canyon de Chelly. There are five awesome scenic overlooks, including the trailhead to beautiful White House Ruin (about 1½ hours' walk, round-trip). Sixteen miles along the drive is Spider Rock, the 800-foot monolith that is the legendary home of Spider Woman, a Navajo diety. Mothers warn their children to be good or Spider Woman will carry them off to her home and devour them.

There are about 2,000 prehistoric sites and 12 major ruins in the national monument. It's believed the Anasazi came here about A.D. 200, and their earliest dwellings were pit houses. About A.D. 1100

(ABOVE) *Navajo routes are sometimes marked with homemade signs and colorful road art.*

(RIGHT) *Navajo sheep on the White House Trail at Canyon de Chelly form an interesting pattern against this scenic tapestry.* KEN AKERS

BELOW) *Lorenzo Hubbell established his famed trading post in 1876. The rustic interior has been little changed since then.* RICHARD EMBERY

White House Ruin, most famous of the 12 major prehistoric cliff dwellings in Canyon de Chelly National Monument, provides a fascinating look at life on the Colorado Plateau many centuries before the white man came. Visitors may walk down to the ruin or view it from the south rim drive.
DICK DIETRICH

(TOP) *Sandstone formations are a common feature of the desolate landscape along Navajo Route 12, near the New Mexico border.*

(ABOVE) *Red Lake offers a welcome scenic contrast to the stark terrain of Navajoland.*

(RIGHT) *Wheatfields Lake, south of Tsaile at a chilly 7,200-feet altitude, offers year-round boating and fishing.* PHOTOS BY KEN AKERS

(OPPOSITE) *Window Rock, capital of the Navajo Nation, derives its name from this nearby stone arch.* JERRY JACKA

they moved into their cliff apartments and remained until a drought caused them to leave late in the 13th century. The Navajo arrived about 1600 (some anthropologists say as early as 1400) and became farmers and shepherds, which they are to this day.

Leaving Chinle, on the western end of the national monument, Navajo Route 64 hugs the north rim of Canyon del Muerto. Along the way are scenic overlooks at Ledge Ruins, Antelope House, Mummy Cave, and Massacre Cave.

Nestled against the majestic backdrop of the Chuska Mountains, a portion of which are called the Lukachukai, is the community of Tsaile and Navajo Community College, America's first Indian-operated college on a reservation. On campus is the Ned A. Hatathli Cultural Center, where Navajo culture and history are preserved.

A 12-mile side trip north from Tsaile on Navajo Route 68 will get you to the Lukachukai Mountains. Ranging up to 10,000 feet, these mountains present a cool green medley of trees. Old-time Navajos believed the Lukachukais "whispered important things" and were the home of spirits to medicine men.

Continuing our tour from Tsaile, take Navajo Route 12 south to Wheatfields Lake. Here, among tall pines at 7,200 feet altitude, is a picnic area with 27 campsites. Boating and fishing are permitted all year.

The highway bends across the New Mexico line south of Wheatfields Lake. Fifteen miles from the lake is a turnoff to the classic old trading post at Crystal, six miles off Navajo Route 12. Established in 1864, it is famous for its Crystal rugs.

Our next stop is Fort Defiance, built in 1851 and the first American military post in what is now Arizona. Colonel Kit Carson used the post during his Canyon de Chelly campaign in 1864, and it later became an Indian agency.

Seven miles south is Window Rock, capital of the Navajo Nation. Near the tribal headquarters building is a small park that features the stone arch for which the Navajo capital is named.

East of the intersection of State Route 264 and Navajo Route 12 is Tse Bonito Park, where hundreds of Navajos were rounded up and held before the historic "Long Walk" to Bosque Redondo, New Mexico, in 1864. Kit Carson led that sorrowful 300-mile trek — one of the major disasters in Navajo-Anglo relations. There is a botanical garden and zoo in the park, and nearby is the Navajo Arts and Crafts Enterprise. the town's only motel is just west of there.

The largest Indian fair in North America is held annually, the first weekend after Labor Day, at the Navajo Nation Fairgrounds, about a half-mile west of the park.

To complete the journey through the Navajo canyonlands, drive 50 miles west on State Route 264, back to Ganado.

— *Marshall Trimble*

Sunset Crater and Wupatki

Our newest volcano • Ruins of ancient towns
Cool forests, grasslands, and a mountain pass

In the winter of A.D. 1064-1065, a volcano erupted northeast of present-day Flagstaff. There are more than 400 volcanic formations in the area, but the others have been dormant for thousands of years.

The volcano built a peak 1,000 feet tall. Devastating lava flows broke from its base and spread east and west. People of the prehistoric Sinagua culture farming the area may have had warning of the eruption, as there is no evidence that many of them died in the conflagration.

About 100 years after the volcano ceased its activity, weather patterns changed and the region experienced an increase in rainfall. The Sinagua returned to farm and the area quickly became one of the Southwest's major population centers.

The Sinagua built many communities north of Sunset Crater. They were joined by other prehistoric peoples, including the Anasazi from the northeast and the Cohonino from the west. Their culture was enriched by visits from the Hohokam of the south, who traded goods from Mexico.

The place now called Wupatki thrived until 1195, but was abandoned between 1215 and 1240. Several other Southwestern cultures vanished or merged about that time because of drought, soil depletion, or perhaps raiding by enemies.

Sunset Crater Volcano National Monument and Wupatki National Monument are connected by a paved loop road from U.S. Route 89 north

(ABOVE) *Cyclists enjoy an outing past cinder cones and grassy meadows to Sunset Crater Volcano National Monument.* ART CLARK

(LEFT) *Sunset Crater, formed some 900 years ago by a volcanic eruption northeast of today's Flagstaff, is one of Arizona's scenic wonders.* JERRY SIEVE

of Flagstaff — one that offers a rewarding day's outing. As a bonus, we'll show you how to end this rich tour with a trip through a mountain pass.

From downtown Flagstaff, travel about 17 miles north on U.S. 89. The Sunset Crater road, beginning the loop, takes off to your right among cinder cones and grassy meadows. It is two miles to the National

Best time to go	March through November
Degree of difficulty	Easy
Type of vehicle	High clearance preferred; sedan can make it
Travel time	Six hours, depending on time spent at two national monuments
Road type	Paved, dirt
Elevation	5,000 - 8,000 feet
Terrain	Forest, mountains
Features	Scenery, hiking, prehistoric cultures

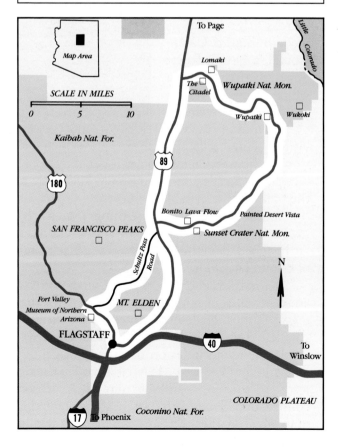

BONITO LAVA FLOW

FROM THE BASE OF SUNSET CRATER
THIS VOLCANIC LAVA EMERGED AND
FILLED THIS VALLEY TO A DEPTH
OF SEVERAL HUNDRED FEET

(ABOVE) *The jagged contours of Bonito Lava Flow at Sunset Crater may be viewed from the lookout or up close from a hiking trail.* WESLEY HOLDEN

(RIGHT) *Just 16 miles beyond Sunset Crater is the Wukoki Ruin at Wupatki National Monument, site of a civilization that thrived here 800 years ago.* DAVID MUENCH

Park Service visitor center for Sunset Crater. Across the road is modern Bonito Campground, a 44-unit Forest Service installation which is open from mid-May through September.

A movie in the visitor center tells the story of Sunset Crater. You can get directions to viewpoints for the crater and Bonito Lava Flow, and the trailhead for Lava Flow Trail.

You can see some of these things from the loop road as it cuts into the side of the volcanic cone. You are hemmed in on the left by the stark, black jumble of Bonito Lava Flow.

Beyond Sunset Crater, the road winds northward and downhill, emerging from pine forest to the sparse grasses of the high desert. Painted Desert Vista is on your left, just four miles beyond Sunset Crater.

It's about 12 miles on to the visitor center at Wupatki. Just before you reach it, a road to the right leads to Wukoki, a striking ruin whose masonry construction blends with the sandstone outcropping from which it rises. Perhaps two or three families

lived in this ruin 800 years ago.

Captain Lorenzo Sitgreaves, one of the first American explorers to cross the plateau, reported on the apparent extent of Wupatki's ruins in 1851: "They are evidently the ruins of a large town, as they occurred at intervals for an extent of eight or nine miles, and the ground was thickly strewed with fragments of pottery in all directions."

The visitor center sits at 4,990 feet, more than 2,000 feet lower than Flagstaff. A trail leads a quarter mile to Wupatki Ruin, the largest of many in the national monument.

Sandstone in this area breaks from ledges in tidy building blocks. The Anasazi may have taught the Sinagua, who earlier lived in pit houses, how to use sandstone in masonry construction. Wupatki was a

four-story pueblo city on a spine of sandstone. It includes a ballcourt contained by low masonry walls not usually found this far north — evidence of influence from Mexico.

About 100 feet east of the ball court, behind the visitor center, is one of the area's "blowholes," geological oddities that puzzle scientists. The holes in the rock surface inhale and exhale air at velocities up to 35 miles per hour. Air flow apparently depends on the difference in air pressure between the earth's surface and subterranean cracks.

A visitor asks, "But where did the Sinagua people get water?"

They stored rainwater and fetched other water long distances in pottery jars and resined baskets. There were a few seeps and springs, but sometimes the people had to carry water from the Little Colorado River, five miles to the northeast.

After the Sinagua vanished, Hopis occupied parts of Wupatki, and so did Navajos. European sheep-herders used the dwellings, and the main Wupatki ruin was so well built that in the 1920s, the first park ranger and his wife lived in it.

Many of the smaller ruins have not been excavated, and are closed to visitors. But as you travel the loop road back to U.S. 89, 12 miles west of the visitor center, you may want to stop for a moment and look at The Citadel, which sits on a butte with a commanding view, and Lomaki, perched on the rim of a box canyon.

You complete the loop by driving south 13 miles on U.S. 89, passing the road you took to Sunset Crater.

About a mile beyond that turnoff, look for an unpaved road to the right and a sign identifying it as the Schultz Pass road, FR 420.

The road climbs from about 7,200 feet to 8,000, passing between the San Francisco Peaks to the north and Mt. Elden and Little Elden to the south. There's some alpine scenery with lots of spring and summer wildflowers to enjoy. Alongside the road, watch for the aspen trees as they turn golden in fall.

The road is a bit rocky near the pass itself, but easily navigated in a passenger car in dry weather. Avoid this leg of the trip in winter. Once over the pass, the road winds down into Fort Valley, just northwest of Flagstaff. Just after the Schultz Pass road joins the Fort Valley road (U.S. Route 180), you'll see the Museum of Northern Arizona on your right. This beautiful museum explores the varied cultures and natural history of the region.

Downtown Flagstaff, your starting point, is a couple of miles south via the Fort Valley road.

— *James E. Cook*

(ABOVE) *Indian legend says this is where the Earth breathes, but modern visitors enjoy leaning over the geologic "blow holes" at Wupatki. They exhale or inhale air at up to 35 mph.* ART CLARK

(LEFT) *Wupatki was a beautiful Sinagua pueblo, four stories high. So sturdily was it built that a park ranger and his wife lived in the ruin eight centuries later.* DICK DIETRICH

Spectacular Sycamore Canyon

White Horse Lake • Sycamore Point • Perkinsville
Verde River • Mingus Mountain • Jerome

Old Bill Williams, the "greatest free trapper of 'em all," roamed these parts in the 1830s. Bill, a tall, skinny, redheaded eccentric, came west as a missionary, but the Indians converted *him*. He had more lives than an alley cat, surviving one hair-raising adventure after another until a Ute war party cut him down in 1849.

The community that grew up 30 miles west of Flagstaff after the railroad came through in the early 1880s was named Williams in his honor. Its proximity to the world's greatest natural architectural masterpiece caused Williams to proclaim itself the "Gateway to the Grand Canyon." Williams is also a gateway to some wonderful back road adventures, including this one south through pine-clad mountains, lakes, and canyons to Jerome, which clings perilously to the slopes of Cleopatra Hill. Plan to spend most of the day. Although the trip is only 75 miles long, 23 miles of it paved, you'll want to "stop and smell the roses" along the way.

Begin at the corner of Bill Williams Avenue and Fourth Street in Williams. Drive south on Fourth Street, which becomes the Perkinsville Road (shown on Forest Service maps as Forest Road 173 at this point), out past the Santa Fe Dam Reservoir, one of seven local fishing lakes.

The first side road you may want to explore is the popular one-hour round-trip drive up Bill Williams Mountain. Turn west on Forest Road 111, some five miles south of town, and follow the cinder-packed road through ponderosa pine to Douglas

fir and aspen — high-country scenery at its best.

Back on the Perkinsville Road, you cross the ranges of the Hat Ranch, part of the old Quarter Circle Double X. This outfit was once owned by Arizona's first congresswoman, Isabella Greenway, wife of General John C. Greenway.

Best time to go	April through November
Degree of difficulty	Moderate
Type of vehicle	High clearance; sedan can make it
Travel time	Six hours; good camping for overnight
Road type	Paved, dirt
Elevation	3,800 - 9,200 feet
Terrain	Forest, mountains
Features	Scenery, history

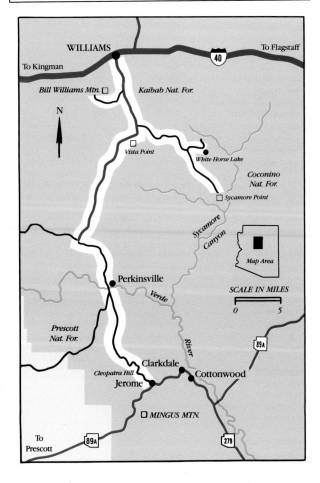

(ABOVE) *Brilliant gaillardia paint the forest landscape near White Horse Lake, southeast of Williams.*
(LEFT) *Bill Williams Mountain, south of Williams, was named for a colorful trapper who roamed these wilds 150 years ago.* BOTH BY BOB AND SUE CLEMENZ

She was a friend of President Franklin D. and Eleanor Roosevelt, who rested up here after the 1932 presidential campaign.

In these mountains you're likely to see mule deer, turkey, Abert squirrels, antelope, rabbits, elk, a variety of birds, and even such elusive critters as bears, lions, foxes, coyotes, and badgers.

Eight miles south of Williams on the Perkinsville Road, take Forest Road 110, a well-maintained dirt road veering east to White Horse Lake and Sycamore Point. Seven miles in on FR 110 is a junction. Turn left on Forest Road 109 and go three miles to beautiful White Horse Lake, called the "Gem of the Kaibab." The lake is stocked with trout, and has bluegill and catfish. The Kaibab National Forest also has campgrounds with 94 units, running water, and boat ramps.

The drive on Forest Road 110 to Sycamore Point, 17 miles from the Perkinsville Road, passes through ponderosa pine and Gambel oak into piñon-juniper country as it approaches Sycamore Canyon. The road leads right to the rim of the canyon, called "Little Grand Canyon" for good reason.

The elevation at the canyon's edge is 7,000 feet, but it drops to 3,600 feet at the bottom. It's a mile wide and extends for 20-some scenic miles. This maze of rocky chasms and red rock formations resembles Oak Creek Canyon, its better-known neighbor, except this is a designated wilderness and has no roads, and relatively few hikers.

Legends persist about lost gold mines in this wild area, one of them supposedly discovered by Spanish soldiers in the 1760s. Marion Perkins, who has lived in these parts all his life, has heard all those lost treasure stories and believes there is some truth to them.

Perkins' grandfather bought the 76 Ranch on the Verde River in 1900. In 1912, the Santa Fe Railroad ran a branch line from Drake east into Clarkdale, put a station on the Perkins ranch, and decided to call it Perkinsville.

Backtracking to the Perkinsville Road we come upon Vista Point, a few miles south. From this lookout you can get an impressive view of Mingus Mountain on the south side of the Verde Valley and the Mogollon Rim country to the east.

From Vista Point, the road begins a long descent toward the Verde River. Twenty-three miles south of Williams is a junction. Take the east fork of Forest Road 492/County Road 71. Here the road turns to dirt and later becomes FR 354/County 70 and finally FR 318/County 72, but it's generally good except in wet weather. The only really rough spot is around Government Canyon as you begin the final descent to the Canyon, the Verde River, and Perkinsville.

(TOP LEFT) *They call it "Arizona's Little Grand Canyon," and Sycamore Canyon richly deserves the name. It's a vast chasm of red rocks and green foliage.*

(TOP RIGHT) *Fishermen and campers love beautiful White Horse Lake, 14 miles west of Sycamore Point.*

(ABOVE) *The stout steel bridge over the Verde River near Perkinsville is a venerable landmark.*

(RIGHT) *Mingus Mountain looms over the Perkins ranch country.*

PHOTOS BY BOB AND SUE CLEMENZ

The old bridge over the Verde is one of those one-lane steel frame rigs. It's another 16 miles to Jerome, up the flanks of the Black Mountains. The road runs atop the old narrow gauge railroad bed from Chino Valley to Jerome. That road, built in 1893 by William Andrews Clark, owner of the United Verde copper mine, was called the "United Verde and Pacific," a rather lofty name since it went only 27 miles.

Approaching a cut through a red-hued ridge, you can pause and look back toward the Perkins ranch and Bill Williams Mountain.

That's a nice preliminary for the next stop, called First View, with a panorama of the entire Verde Valley, Mogollon Rim, Sycamore and Oak Creek canyons, San Francisco Peaks, and the old boom town of Jerome. You'll find that late afternoon is the best time to see it, and this is a wonderful place to end your trip.

But wait — there are two encores. Drop into Jerome and plan to spend some time in Arizona's "liveliest ghost town." And lastly, four miles below at Clarkdale, is the Verde River Canyon Excursion Train which winds it's way from Clarkdale along the Verde River Canyon to Perkinsville and back. Travelers will see a myriad of scenery and riparian wildlife, but be sure to call ahead for reservations.

— *Marshall Trimble*

(TOP LEFT) *The Verde River Canyon Excursion Train provides passengers with a tour of one of central Arizona's most scenic areas.*

(TOP RIGHT) *Jerome is famed as a ghost town, but tourism has brought this corpse back to life.*

(ABOVE) *The restored library of the Jerome State Historic Park, preserves the lifestyle of the copper barons.*

(OPPOSITE) *Memorabilia of the days when Jerome was a rip-roarin' copper camp are on display in the Jerome State Historic Park in the foreground of this panorama of the Verde Valley.* PHOTOS BY BOB AND SUE CLEMENZ

Schnebly Hill - Stoneman Lake

Breathtaking views of Sedona and Oak Creek Canyon • Grassy parks
Mormon Lake • Spring and summer wildflowers

The usual way to admire the startling red rock spires and buttes in the Sedona area is from below, with head tilted back and mind searching for words to describe them.

But there is a relatively easy way to get a panoramic view of Sedona and Oak Creek Canyon from above. The Schnebly Hill Road can be the start of a cool loop trip through forest, meadows, and past a couple of pretty lakes — a memorable adventure.

At Exit 298 on Interstate 17, just 100 miles north of Phoenix, take State Route 179 to Sedona, starting point for this tour. Not quite 15 miles along this paved highway, a bridge crosses Oak Creek into the original part of Sedona. Instead of crossing that bridge, go straight ahead (north) and you are on the Schnebly Hill Road (also called Forest Road 153), named for pioneer T. C. Schnebly.

This was a cow trail once, built by the pioneer Munds family to move cattle from winter pasture in the Verde Valley to summer range on top of the Mogollon Plateau. It was upgraded to a road early in this century, giving Verde Valley residents a shorter trip to Flagstaff. Before that, they had to go by the old Stoneman Road, which we'll get to shortly. The Schnebly Hill route was replaced about 1914 by the Oak Creek Canyon road (State Route 89A) — shorter still — but Schnebly Hill continues to be a popular scenic road.

Paved for the first mile, it then becomes a graded dirt road that demands a driver's attention. It climbs out through Bear Wallow Canyon and begins twisting

(LEFT) Admire the red rock wonderland of Sedona and Oak Creek Canyon, with its fantastic spires and formations, from above while driving Schnebly Hill Road. This view is an artist's dream: rocks of multi-colored hues, green backdrop, clear blue sky, and marshmallow white clouds. DICK CANBY

up the face of the hill. Although the road looks dangerous, the uphill lane hugs the cut most of the distance, rather than treading the brink of space. You can get your first overviews of the Sedona area from narrow turnouts.

It is six miles to the top and Schnebly Hill Vista. This viewpoint is a little over 6,000 feet elevation, about 1,800 feet higher than Sedona. Here you'll get a spectacular look at the mouth of Oak Creek Canyon, with Steamboat Rock guarding it on the west. Below and beyond Steamboat lie the older "downtown" Sedona and West Sedona. The view stretches on to Mingus Mountain on the west side of

Best time to go	April through November
Degree of difficulty	Moderate
Type of vehicle	High clearance; sedan can make it
Travel time	Six hours; good camping for overnight
Road type	Dirt, some pavement
Elevation	4,000 - 7,000 feet
Terrain	Mountain, forest
Features	Scenery, history, fishing

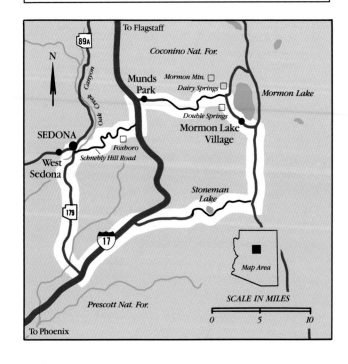

the Verde Valley. Now it's time to look down on the view and think of appropriate words. "Breathtaking," perhaps?

The vista is at the very edge of northeastern Arizona's plateau region, and botanists call this a "transition zone." As the Schnebly Hill Road continues eastward, prickly pear and century plant mingle with junipers, and the first pine trees.

Soon the road meanders through a ponderosa pine forest and skirts "parks" like that at the old ranch called Foxboro, four miles beyond the viewpoint. These grassy clearings are called cienegas in eastern Arizona, and meadows elsewhere. But in this part of the world they are parks, and you'll see several of them on this trip.

Three miles beyond Foxboro, the road ends at Interstate 17. Take the freeway two miles north and exit at Munds Park (named for the same ranching family). Turn right on Pinewood Boulevard past the country club and through the attractive residence area at Pinewood.

After about a mile, the road becomes unpaved Coconino National Forest Road 240. Not all junctions are clearly marked, so follow the obviously most-traveled road and watch for mileage signs to Mormon Lake Village, 15 miles from Pinewood.

A few aspens appear among the pine and oak as the road skirts 8,440-foot Mormon Mountain and the lake comes into view.

Mormon Lake occupies a large basin which has been alternately wet and dry. Pioneer Mormon dairymen used it for a pasture beginning in 1876, and there is a theory that trampling by cattle sealed the soil and made it hold water, except in periods of prolonged drought.

The water's ebb and flow never kept Mormon Lake from being a popular recreation spot. Forest Service campgrounds with a combined total of 64 family units are located at Dairy Springs and Double Springs. They lie beside Forest Road 90, which curves around the west side of the lake.

Turn right and follow FR90 through Mormon Lake Village to where it connects with Forest Highway 3. Turn right and drive south on FH3 through the pines and several parks painted with spring and summer wildflowers.

Eight miles south of Mormon Lake turn right and you'll be on historic, unpaved Stoneman Lake Road.

An aerial view of Schnebly Hill, where spectacular vistas abound. DICK CANBY

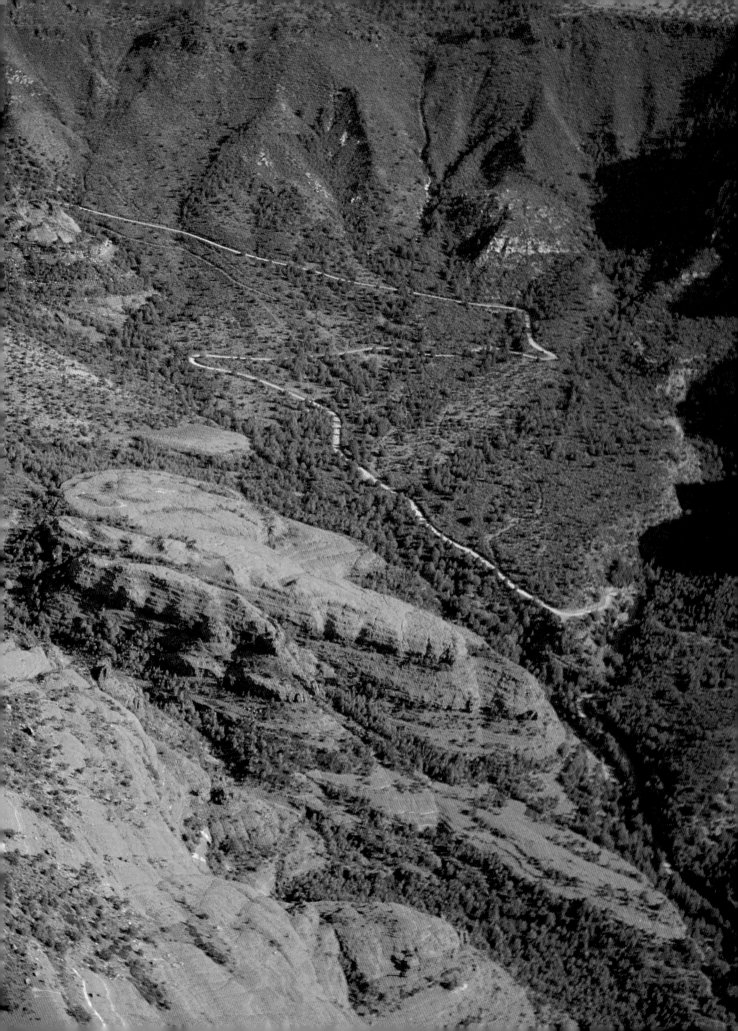

(TOP) *From the 6,000-foot crest of Schnebly Hill, you can see the trees below ignite in a blaze of color in early fall.* DICK CANBY

(ABOVE) *Verdant "parks" such as this one at Foxboro Lake, four miles beyond the crest, dot the ponderosa forest above Oak Creek Canyon.* WESLEY HOLDEN

(LEFT) *The rock garage at Foxboro Lake is a crumbling reminder of earlier days when the woods rang with voices of children from a nearby summer camp.*

(OPPOSITE PAGE, TOP) *Stoneman Lake, east of Interstate 17, is one of Arizona's few natural lakes.* BOTH BY DICK CANBY

(OPPOSITE PAGE, CENTER) *Wildflowers bloom along the Stoneman Lake Road.*

(OPPOSITE PAGE, BOTTOM) *Mormon Lake's spacious campground is a cool summer haven for fishermen and lovers of the outdoors.*
BOTH BY WESLEY HOLDEN

One of Arizona's first roads came through here in the 1860s, leading from New Mexico to the territorial capital at Prescott. It was called the Chavez Road, and sometimes the Stoneman Road. Accounts of its rigors appear in the writings of frontier soldiers and civilians, but the road has been tamed now.

Stoneman Lake, which sits in a small bowl, is one of the few "natural" lakes in Arizona. It was named for General George Stoneman, commander of the Military Department of Arizona in the 1860s and 1870s. About six miles after you leave Forest Highway 3, a pullout beside the road gives you a scenic view of the little lake from above.

Not quite a mile farther along Forest Road 213, a side road leads to the lake, to the summer homes on the shore, and to trout fishing.

Not far beyond that side road, Road 213 makes the transition back into junipers, and the pavement begins at the Coconino-Yavapai county line. Within 15 minutes, you're back to Interstate 17.

The lower end of the Stoneman Lake Road, and Interstate 17 going toward Phoenix, offer other commanding views of the Verde Valley.

If it's scenic beauty you crave, far from the crowds and the heat of the desert country, with a bit of history to spice the trip, the road up Schnebly Hill and over to Mormon and Stoneman lakes is for you.

— *James E. Cook*

Charming Cherry

**A nostalgic little trip to yesterday • Rural beauty • Verde Valley vistas
Historic Cherry • Mile-high forest and rangeland**

Cherry is a delightful little community that looks like it was scooped out of some 19th century rural landscape by a giant prospector's shovel and tucked away in this picturesque little Yavapai County canyon. Driving in from either direction, you "come around the bend" and this lush, green valley suddenly materializes in front of you.

Cherry is one of those obvious place names. Prospectors found wild cherry trees growing along the creek and dubbed their community accordingly. Ironically, a few years later the Norville Cherry family of Texas took up residence here, thus leading to some confusion about the origin of the place name.

This area isn't far, about 10 miles as the crow flies, from the fabulously rich mines at old Jerome. During the late 1870s, mule-powered arrastras were used to reduce the gold ore from the mines in the neighborhood of Cherry.

The town's heyday came around 1907 when six mills were grinding up the gold-rich ore dug from the nearby hills. The boom didn't last long, however, and the total recorded production amounted to only some $100,000 mostly in gold.

The area was rich in surface ores — something that prompted several promotional schemes. The Pfau Mine won dubious notoriety when its promoters salted it and then attempted to hornswoggle world-famous engineer John Hays Hammond. (Hammond figured out the scam and didn't buy.)

Old Man Bunker's dairy cow wins the utilitarian award around these parts. Each day Bunker milked the animal before breakfast, then rode her up to his mine, where she was used as a beast of burden to haul ore. That evening he rode her back down the mountain where Bossy was milked again for supper.

There are three ways to get to Cherry from Phoenix. The first and easiest way is to go north on Interstate 17 to State Route 169 (Cherry Road), which is 17 miles north of Cordes Junction. Go west 5.3 miles to the sign pointing you north along a pleasant six-mile dirt road to Cherry.

The second way is to go north on Interstate 17 to Verde Valley. At State Route 260, turn west four miles toward Cottonwood, then turn south on the 12-mile dirt road to Cherry. You'll make a steep climb out of the Verde Valley. The road is excellent and well-maintained, but avoid it in wet weather.

The third approach into Cherry is from Dewey, a town on State Route 69. Take State Route 169 at its junction with Route 69 and drive northeast.

Best time to go	All year
Degree of difficulty	Easy
Type of vehicle	Family car
Travel time	Six hours
Road type	Paved, dirt
Elevation	1,100 - 5,000 feet
Terrain	Grassland, mountain
Features	Scenery, history

A straw-filled resident guards a summer garden in the quiet community of Cherry. At just over 5,000 feet elevation, the tiny town enjoys a benign climate and is a perfect retreat from life's hectic pace. JAMES TALLON

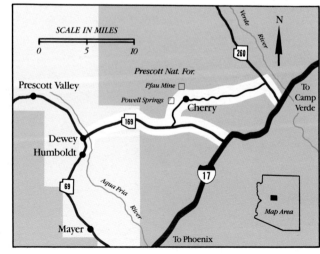

(TOP LEFT) *A cool forest hideaway: Powell Springs Campground along the road to Cherry.*

(LEFT) *Rocky Mountain mule deer abound in the area.*

(BOTTOM LEFT) *Folks in Cherry have plenty of privacy, and the great outdoors for their back yard.*

(INSET) *Yellow tombstone roses add to Cherry's abundant beauty.*

(RIGHT) *Along a peaceful country lane in Cherry, mailboxes await word from the outside world.*

PHOTOS BY JAMES TALLON

But first, you might want to pause here for a short but interesting side trip. A few yards east of this junction, on the west bank of the Agua Fria River, is a piece of the historic Black Canyon Highway. This stretch of dirt road leads south into Humboldt. Less than a mile down this road, in a cow pasture on the west side, are the rocky ruins of an old stage station. This was also the ranch home of King Woolsey, one of Arizona's legendary Indian fighters in the 1860s. From this place, Woolsey led several civilian expeditions against Yavapai and Tonto Apache raiders.

It takes only a few minutes to complete this little back road trip between Dewey and Humboldt, but it's well worth the time.

Now back to Dewey and Highway 169. From Dewey to the Cherry turnoff is 9.5 miles. The flora along Cherry Road is low-slung chaparral, mostly scrub oak and manzanita. After a couple of miles, ponderosa pines and live oak become dominant.

For those who care to spend the night in the outdoors, four miles north of State Route 169 is a sign pointing west to the campground at Powell Springs. This mile-high campground is .3 mile west of Cherry Road. You'll find 14 campsites with benches, tables, firepits, and barbecues. A usually-dry wash runs next to the campground, but a hand-cranked pump will provide an ample supply of drinking water. There is a 14-day camping limit.

The road leading into the community of Cherry resembles a midwest country lane. A bird's-eye vista of the tree-lined creek gives the appearance of a giant green serpent winding its way down the canyon.

Cherry would be an ideal place to visit in the fall when the leaves turn, transforming our green reptile into a variegated profusion of colors. Cherry, apple, peach, and pear trees thrive in this little valley.

Cherry Creek is what the Indians refer to as "upside down" because, like many creeks and rivers in this state, a good part of it runs underground.

Perhaps the oldest building in Cherry is the venerable stage-stop residence, occupied since the mid-1860s. Cherry's population is about 50 permanent residents and another 15 who live here part-time. The town's major social event of the year is a Fourth of July community picnic. Now you can't get much more old-fashioned than that!

Driving north from Cherry, you'll climb out of the narrow canyon and top out on the crest. It's a good place to pull over and look back for a last appreciative view of Cherry.

Off to the north is a breathtaking panorama of the Verde Valley. Far to the west is the country around Perkinsville, Jerome, and Sycamore Canyon. Out front are the red buttes of Oak Creek Canyon. Winding its way across this vast valley, the Verde River meanders southward toward its rendezvous with the Salt River. Looming majestically in the background are the San Francisco Peaks, the loftiest in all Arizona.

All in all, the trip to Cherry is a little jewel.

— *Marshall Trimble*

Tour 7: 60 Miles, Starts from Camp Verde

Childs, Irving, and Fossil Creek

A remote Eden on the Verde River • Fort Verde
Rustic hot springs • The long view from Ikes Backbone

In the unwritten lore of Arizona, Childs is a name dropped by geographic social climbers. It represents true remoteness, a place visited only by those who really want to get there.

However, it is no longer that difficult to reach the secluded oasis on the Verde River.

The Verde is one of Arizona's half-dozen major rivers. It has its origin north of Prescott, and drains the large Verde Valley to the east. Leaving the southeast corner of the valley, it slices through the mountains, eventually joining the Salt River a few miles east of Phoenix.

This trip starts in the laid-back town of Camp Verde, which started life as a military outpost in the 1860s and '70s, one which was critical to General George Crook's campaign against Apaches and Yavapais. While you're there, you might want to visit Fort Verde State Historic Park in the center of town. The old parade ground and some of the officers quarters still exist, and there's a lively small museum in a former post administration building.

Follow the main street of Camp Verde, State Route 260, out the south end of town, across the Verde River bridge. For the first few miles you stay on State Route 260, which follows historic Crook's Trail, the wagon road built by the general in 1872. Five miles out of Camp Verde, where the road crosses West Clear Creek, the Coconino National Forest maintains a shady campground with 20 developed sites.

Look sharp about a mile beyond Clear Creek because the road you need to take, the Fossil Creek road, is not well marked. As the pavement bends left, the unpaved Fossil Creek road departs to the right, and immediately descends a bluff.

The road is well-maintained, but its twisting course makes it slow going. It crosses several watershed divides, dropping first into Sycamore Creek, one of several by that name in Arizona; then into the basin of Hackberry Creek, again one of several places by that name; and then into Cimarron Basin.

You'll be traveling along the lower edge of the transition zone between chaparral brushlands and the higher-growing cedars, junipers, and piñons.

Best time to go	March through November
Degree of difficulty	Moderate; never in rain
Type of vehicle	High clearance; sedan can make it
Travel time	Five hours
Road type	Paved, dirt; blind curves
Elevation	5,000 - 7,000 feet
Terrain	Mountains, forest
Features	Scenery, history

(ABOVE) *The Fossil Creek road meanders among rolling hills southeast of Camp Verde.*

OPPOSITE PAGE: (CLOCKWISE FROM TOP)
Officers' quarters at Fort Verde State Historic Park look much the same today as when General George Crook and his staff occupied them.

The commanding officer's dining room.

Territorial cavalrymen processed paper work in this office.

The commander's parlor offered pleasant amenities.
PHOTOS BY BOB AND SUZANNE CLEMENZ

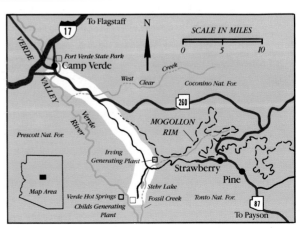

Towering golden-topped century plants were blooming on our trip there, and mesquite trees were loaded with pods of beans. This was a traditional food for Native Americans before other sources of flour were available, and also helped keep their livestock alive.

About 10 miles along the road, where it is flanked by two stone buttes, Towel Creek Trail leaves the road on the right. It will lead hikers to the Verde River, six miles west.

The creek got its name in 1901 when cowboy Charlie Wingfield, getting ready for a rodeo, lost a new towel in the creek. Charlie's bellyaching about the loss caused his buddy to call it Towel Creek. It was officially "Taul Creek" on maps, until cartographers realized that was the southwestern cowboy's pronunciation of "towel."

Thirteen miles from the pavement, as the road drops into the Fossil Creek drainage, turn right onto the road to Childs. For the first part of the six-mile trip, you'll parallel Fossil Creek, named because its travertine content coats objects in the water.

Originally, the creek was fed by Fossil Springs, a 20,000-gallons-per-minute water source in the mountains to the east. The creek drops 1,600 feet in its 10-mile trip to the Verde River.

Early in this century, the springs' output was tapped for Arizona's first hydroelectric power. Electricity was needed for the town of Prescott and for the growing mining town of Jerome. Entrepreneurs built the hydroelectric plant on the banks of the Verde, and built a seven-mile flume to carry water from Fossil Springs. The complex was a monumental construction task, using the energies of 600 men and 450 mules. Although the plant is now obsolete, it is paid for and it just keeps running; the nation's mechanical engineers have designated it one of their historic landmarks.

The flume parallels your route as the road climbs the east side of Ikes Backbone to Ike Saddle. As the road crosses through the saddle to the west side of the mountain, you suddenly face a spectacular view of the Verde River canyon below, and the tiny collection of buildings know as Childs. The road drops from about 4,000 feet in the saddle to 3,000 at the river, winding for two miles in the process.

The power plant and the oasis where its workers live are closed to the public, but a rough road to the left takes you to the river bank. There is an undeveloped campground here, with only primitive restrooms.

The Verde, which is between gorges at this point, flows serenely by; clear waters of Fossil Springs, having left the turbines, mingle with the Verde at your feet. It's an ideal spot for a picnic or for overnight camping.

A sign shows the trail to Verde Hot Springs, one mile upstream. There used to be a resort hotel there,

and legend says it was built in the 1920s, during Prohibition, so that Arizonans of means could party in private. The resort burned in 1962, and its ruins and the road have since been obliterated. Hikers must wade the river a couple times to reach its two natural hot tubs, one in a tiny stone building, the other in the open air.

Climbing back over Ike Saddle on the return trip, you'll see a small lake to your right. It's called Stehr Lake. There are undeveloped Forest Service camping sites along the shore and a few bass, sunfish, and carp in the lake.

As you reach the Camp Verde-Fossil Creek road, turn right instead of left. It's two miles to another Arizona Public Service hydro station at Irving on

(TOP LEFT) *The power plant at Childs, built more than eight decades ago, was Arizona's first hydroelectric generator.*

(ABOVE) *Hikers pause to photograph the tail race pool below the Childs power plant. More than a million gallons an hour rush through turbines and into the Verde River.*

(RIGHT) *Few Arizonans know about Verde Hot Springs, a one-mile hike upstream from Childs, where resort guests of an earlier era relaxed and forgot their cares.* PHOTOS BY BOB AND SUE CLEMENZ

(LEFT) *Farther down the Fossil Creek road is the Irving hydroelectric plant. Along with the Childs plant, it provided much of the electric power for Phoenix in the 1920s. But then Phoenix had only 30,000 residents in those days.*

(LOWER LEFT) *This flume was built 90 years ago to transport water from Fossil Springs. The country surrounding it is some of the most pristine wilderness in Arizona.*

(RIGHT) *You'll come upon an old swimmin' hole, just like grandpa remembers so fondly, complete with rope swing. It's on Fossil Creek, not far from Irving.*
PHOTOS BY
BOB AND SUE CLEMENZ

Fossil Creek. The plant was built so generators could use the waters of Fossil Springs twice. In the 1920s, the Childs-Irving complex provided much of the energy needed by Phoenix, then a town of about 30,000 people.

There's a parking lot just beyond the Irving compound, and it's the hiker's trailhead for Fossil Springs, four miles upstream; along with Fossil Springs Wilderness and the Flume Road, used to build the flume about 1909.

Since the 1920s, a road has gone east from this point up Fossil Creek Hill, 4.5 miles of switchbacks climbing 1,600 feet. For many years, this was the main route between the Verde Valley and the Strawberry-Pine-Payson area. It connects with Arizona Route 87 in Strawberry.

Rock slides occasionally close the road between Irving and Strawberry. As of this writing, it had just been reopened after being closed several months. The trip to Strawberry is a good drive for people who like mountain scenery and don't mind a very narrow dirt road with lots of high, airy switchbacks.

For the rest, it's a slow but easy jaunt back to Camp Verde the way you came. And you will be among the "upwardly mobile" who can say they have actually been to Childs.

— *James E. Cook*

Old Rim Road

**Mountain viewpoints • Lakes and streams • Wild game and wildflowers
Crook's Trail • A funnel of history**

To paraphrase a notion recently expressed by one Arizona writer: If the Mogollon Rim were in a less scenic region, it might be a national park.

The Mogollon Escarpment runs diagonally across Arizona from its waistline at the New Mexico border to the area of Lake Mead. It is not always visible as a rim. But for one 42-mile stretch, between Arizona Routes 87 and 260, the Rim is a bold parapet, rising as much as 2,000 feet above the Tonto Basin.

Concentrated along this stretch are:

- Some of the longest, prettiest views in Arizona.
- Rich history, much of it the history of violence and conquest.
- Lush forests of pine, spruce, several kinds of fir, oak, fern, and wildflowers, populated by elk, deer, wild turkeys, and occasionally a bear or mountain lion.
- Secluded mountain lakes of quiet beauty.

In 1871, Captain John G. Bourke, aide to General George Crook, described the Rim as "a strange freak of nature, a mountain canted on one side."

We owe much to his commander, who in 1872 had a wagon road built along the crest of the Rim to connect Fort Apache, Camp Verde, and Whipple Barracks at Prescott (see Tour No. 9). Crook's road has been improved several times. Now designated Forest Road 300, the Rim Road, it is your passage to some of the most rewarding sightseeing in Arizona.

This is a warm-weather trip, best from mid-May to early October. While there are several ways to approach it, one of the best is to use Payson as the starting point for a loop trip.

Go north 27 miles from Payson on State Route 87, past Pine and Strawberry, to the Rim Road turnoff. It turns right off the highway, starts a bit rough, but

(LEFT) *Sunrise over the sheer Mogollon Rim is not soon forgotten.*

(FAR LEFT) *The Old Rim Road, which once rang with the shouts of General George Crook's Indian fighters, offers some of the most dramatic panoramas in all Arizona.*
PHOTOS BY JEFF KIDA

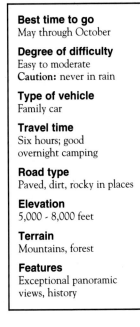

Best time to go
May through October

Degree of difficulty
Easy to moderate
Caution: never in rain

Type of vehicle
Family car

Travel time
Six hours; good
overnight camping

Road type
Paved, dirt, rocky in places

Elevation
5,000 - 8,000 feet

Terrain
Mountains, forest

Features
Exceptional panoramic
views, history

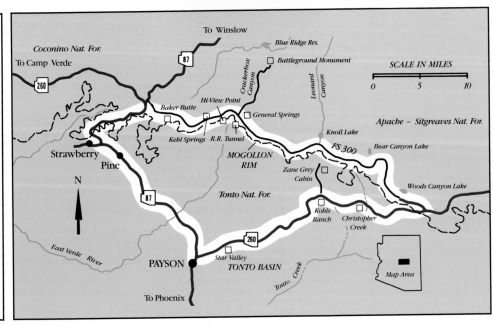

improves from west to east. Sandstone pops through the road surface in several places, but we picked our way across it carefully in a low-slung Buick Regal.

This region offers one of the most varied assortments of trees and plants in Coconino National Forest. Ferns give a jungle effect, and wildflowers are profuse in spring and after late summer rains.

Watch for white chevrons tacked to some ponderosa pines: They mark the route of Crook's Trail.

Five miles east of Baker Butte, the Kehl Springs campground occupies a shady glen covered with ferns and tall grasses. The campground is enclosed by a split rail fence that dates back at least 50 years.

As the road finds its way back out to the brink of the Rim, you can glimpse ranches and clearings in the Tonto Basin far below. Resist the temptation to stop in the roadway; there is quite a lot of traffic at times.

Two miles beyond Kehl Springs is Hi-View Point, the most photographed scenic overlook on the Rim. You can pull out here and look over a lot of Arizona, including the rooftops of Payson to the south. It was probably the view from this point that caused Martha Summerhayes, a young Army wife, to recall after her hard trip across the Rim in 1874: "I remember thinking, as we alighted from our ambulances and stood looking over the Basin, 'Surely I have never seen anything to compare with this — but oh! would any sane human being voluntarily go through what I have endured on this journey, in order to look on this wonderful scene?' "

(ABOVE) *Baker Lake, on the western end of the Rim Road, looks more like a meadow today, but in the 1870s it was a source of water for cavalry horses.*

(INSET) *A lonely headstone stands where Andres Moreno, a freighter and former member of Arizona's first militia was murdered in 1887.* PHOTOS BY WESLEY HOLDEN

(LEFT) *Martha Summerhayes, more than a century ago, said of the Rim Road view, "Surely I have never seen anything to compare with this!"* JEFF KIDA

While the Rim drops abruptly into the Tonto Basin on the south, the plateau to the north is cut with a grid of deep canyons. Their streams flow northward into the Little Colorado River, and several offer good trout fishing.

From the head of Crackerbox Canyon, 11 miles east of State Route 87, a side road goes north seven miles to the Battleground Monument. On July 17, 1882, several troops of U.S. cavalry converged on 60 Indians who had been raiding ranches and towns across east-central Arizona Territory. The Battle of Big Dry Wash, which broke organized Apache resistance to the white man's intrusion, is commemorated by a bronze-on-sandstone monument.

The last mile of road to the monument is rocky, and where it ends, a foot trail leads a quarter mile to the monument. We saw six elk and four whitetail does in Crackerbox Canyon and on the adjacent Battleground Ridge.

The water you see in the canyon north of the monument is Blue Ridge Reservoir, best reached from the north side by another road off State Route 87.

Now return to the Rim Road, which next drops into the notch at the head of General Springs Canyon, lowest point on the Rim for many miles, and a funnel of history. In 1883, the Mineral Belt Railroad tried to tunnel through the Rim here to put a railroad between Globe and Flagstaff. The project failed, but the supply road became an important route off the Rim for Tonto Basin pioneers. A trail leads down to the remnants of the tunnel.

COCONINO National Forest

MOGOLLON RIM

THE MOGOLLON RIM IS A STEEP ESCARPMENT MARKING THE SOUTHERN EDGE OF THE COLORADO PLATEAU. THE PLATEAU EXTENDS NORTH AND EAST INTO UTAH, COLORADO AND NEW MEXICO. IN THIS AREA THE RIM IS A RESULT OF UPLIFT ALONG THE NORTH SIDE OF AN EAST-WEST TRENDING FAULT AND THE REMOVAL OF ABOUT 2500 FEET OF PALEOZOIC AGE SEDIMENTARY ROCKS FROM THE UPLIFTED EDGE OF THE PLATEAU. THIS EROSION HAS CAUSED THE RIM TO RECEDE ABOUT 7 MILES FROM THE FAULT SINCE THE INITIAL UPLIFT OCCURRED 15 TO 20 MILLION YEARS AGO. THIS MOVEMENT WAS FOLLOWED BY VOLCANIC ACTIVITY WHICH SPREAD LAVA OVER THE PLATEAU AND RIM IN SEVERAL PLACES SUCH AS BAKER BUTTE.

U. S. DEPARTMENT OF AGRICULTURE

(TOP LEFT) *Ambitious Arizonans tried unsuccessfully to tunnel through the Mogollon Rim near General Springs in 1883 to run a railroad down through Payson to the mines at Globe. The results of their efforts are still visible today.* WESLEY HOLDEN

(BOTTOM LEFT) *Forest greenery makes this drive a delight.*

(RIGHT) *Was the Garden of Eden more entrancing than this pristine scene of ferns at dawn on the Rim Road?*

(BELOW) *Woods Canyon Lake, at the east end of the Rim Road, is one of Arizona's favorite trout fishing lakes.* PHOTOS BY JEFF KIDA

Half a mile north of the Rim Road is General Springs Cabin, a historic former fire guard station which the Coconino National Forest has restored to resemble its original 1915 appearance. There are several viewpoints in the next few miles. An occasional blue-colored Engelmann spruce stands out among other conifers.

Several canyons north of the Rim have been dammed to create fishing lakes. One of the prettiest is Knoll Lake in Leonard Canyon, 77 acres impounded in 1963. The turnoff is nine miles east of General Springs. Knoll Lake campground has 42 campsites.

From Leonard Canyon, it's another eight miles to the turnoff for Bear Canyon Lake, and nine miles beyond that is the turnoff to popular Woods Canyon Lake. Both have large, developed campgrounds.

The Rim Road is paved beginning at the Woods Canyon turnoff. It is three miles on to State Route 260 and the 32-mile trip back to Payson to complete the loop. As the highway drops off the Rim, it offers yet another view of the east end of Tonto Basin.

Kohl's Ranch, 12 miles from the Rim, is a historic resort built in 1920. Author Zane Grey's cabin on nearby Tonto Creek was destroyed by a forest fire in 1990, but efforts are underway to collect money for rebuilding the popular tourist attraction.

Grey lived here early in this century, and he based several of his novels in this Rim country. By now, you'll understand why.
— *James E. Cook*

(TOP LEFT) *Several steak houses in the Rim area, such as this one at Christopher Creek, offer tasty fare centered around cowboy steaks and beans.*

(CENTER LEFT) *The awesome Rim towers over travelers driving through the Christopher Creek area.*
PHOTOS BY WESLEY HOLDEN

(BOTTOM LEFT) *Horton Springs, the headwaters of Horton Creek, are the destination for a popular Rim country hike. Find the Horton Creek Trailhead at Upper Tonto Creek Campground, north of Kohl's Ranch.* NICK BEREZENKO

(THIS PAGE) *At Payson, old-time fiddlers vie in summer competition while folks enjoy dancing, both square and round.*
PHOTOS BY JEFF KIDA

Bradshaw Mountain Adventure

Bumble Bee, Crown King, and Horsethief Basin • Cool mountain grandeur
An 'impossible railroad' • Gold mines • Hassayampa Lake

If these old Bradshaw Mountains could talk, they'd tell a mighty colorful story of boisterous, devil-may-care towns with whimsical names such as Bumble Bee, Big Bug, Oro Belle, and Tip Top.

They were peopled mostly by tough hardrock miners and bewhiskered burro men. Each new strike brought claims of great riches guaranteed to fill a prospector's poke sack with nuggets.

Today, it's pretty quiet up here. Gone are the sounds of mining and the lonesome whistle of steam locomotives chugging their way up the mountain to Crown King.

But these narrow, winding roads that weave their way through the Bradshaws can lead you down a nostalgic path into yesteryear, while at the same time taking you through some mighty pretty forest country.

We begin our journey at Exit 248 (Bumble Bee and Crown King), four miles north of Black Canyon City on Interstate 17. A winding dirt road, Forest Road 259, leads six miles down into Bumble Bee — a quiet place these days. Four well-groomed cabins are perched beside the road, and the old schoolhouse on the east side has been converted into a residence. The owners refurbished part of the interior and opened, on a seasonal basis, the Bumble Bee Trading Post.

The general store, once the hub of activity, is abandoned. The ramshackle buildings behind it are the remains of a latter-day developer's rendition of a frontier town. Bumble Bee got its name in 1863 when a prospector tangled with a swarm of the feisty critters. This was not really a boom town, but a station on the historic Black Canyon stagecoach line.

Five miles beyond Bumble Bee, the road forks.

Best time to go	March through November
Degree of difficulty	Demanding
Type of vehicle	High clearance
Travel time	Eight hours; good camping for overnight
Road type	Dirt, rocky in places
Elevation	2,500 - 7,000 feet
Terrain	Desert to forest
Features	Scenery, historic sites

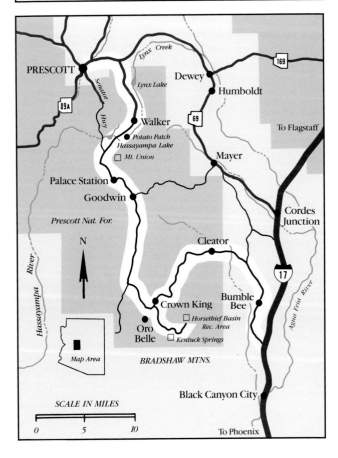

(ABOVE) *Downtown Cleator is not exactly metropolitan; therein lies its charm.*

(LEFT) *Switchbacks, rough roads, and steep grades make the journey up the Bradshaw Mountains to Crown King a demanding adventure.*
PHOTOS BY JAMES TALLON

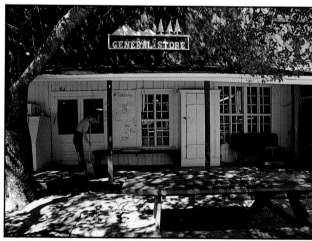

(OPPOSITE PAGE) *The Old West, with saloons and all the trimmings, comes to life at Crown King in the southern Bradshaws. Inside the general store, you'll find almost everything you need, including a post office.*

(ABOVE) *The majestic panorama of the Bradshaw Mountains, as seen from Pine Flat, begs to be photographed.*

(INSET) *There are many abandoned gold mines in the Bradshaws. Exploring them can be dangerous!*
JAMES TALLON PHOTOS

Take the left road past Turkey Creek and two gold mines, the Golden Turkey and Golden Belt. Back in the 1860s, prospectors named this place after the wild turkeys which were abundant. A post office was established in 1869, and a stage station provided primitive comforts to passengers.

Turkey Creek boomed in 1903 when the railroad reached the site. Two years later Jim Cleator arrived and went into business. In 1925, the town's name was changed to Cleator. On one trip through Cleator I met Tom Cleator, son of old Jim and colorful proprietor of the Cleator Store. Bewhiskered Tom lived here for more than 60 years and told fascinating stories about the area until his death a few years ago. The store is still open occasionally (usually on weekends) and a stop here is a must.

The road through here is washboarded and it's difficult to imagine a railroad penetrating this maze of twisting, steep-sided canyons. But around the turn of the century one did just that — an extension of the Prescott and Eastern Railroad, better remembered as "Frank Murphy's Impossible Bradshaw Mountain Railroad."

Murphy, one of Arizona Territory's greatest

(ABOVE) *A highlight of the Bradshaw Mountains trip is a visit to Palace Station, a well-preserved stagecoach stop built in 1874.* JAMES TALLON

(RIGHT) *Hassayampa Lake, near the end of this journey, is a bright jewel in a setting of forest greenery.* ROBERT J. FARRELL

entrepreneurs and visionaries, built the road to bring machinery in to the mines and to haul the ore out. He recruited husky gandy dancers and steel drivers from the East and paid them a dollar a day — twice the going rate — to set grades and lay track. Between 1901 and 1904, they ran a railroad that "couldn't be built" up the back of the mountains that "couldn't be climbed."

The road to Crown King runs atop this old railroad bed. These days, Crown King is a far cry from its boisterous era as a mining center and railroad terminus. During the 1890s, 17 men were killed here, mostly in arguments over women.

The town's store houses the post office and also sells gasoline. Two friendly eating establishments offer good food. Don't miss the historic photographs on the walls of the Crown King Saloon.

A mile west of Crown King, a road to the left (Forest Road 52) heads up a six-mile climb to the Horsethief Basin Recreation Area. About halfway there is a spectacular observation point that looks off to the west. Horsethief Basin (elevation 7,000 feet) was named for the notorious bands of rustlers

who hid and re-branded their stolen livestock here. It's said they drove horses here from southern Utah and, in a grand gesture of fair play, stole cattle here and sold them up north.

For years this was a favorite summer playground for Phoenix residents. Its facilities have decayed somewhat, but wilderness hiking trails abound, and behind a masonry dam are the placid waters of Horsethief Lake. Hazlett Hollow and Kentuck Springs campgrounds have 15 campsites each, and at Kentuck, there is no fee charged.

From the Crown King-Horsethief Basin junction, turn right and it's 18 miles of rough dirt road to Goodwin. The scenery is spectacular and there are plenty of side roads to explore. Goodwin is marked on maps, but there is very little trace of the town named for Arizona's first resident territorial governor, John Goodwin.

About three miles north of the junction at Goodwin is historic Palace Station, a cabin built in 1874 as a way station for stagecoach passengers. From the junction about three miles beyond Palace Station, the Senator Highway (the left fork) will take you past the old Senator Mine and into downtown Prescott. But our journey leads down the right fork, on Forest Road 197, toward the old mining town of Walker. A narrow road heads past beautiful Hassayampa Lake.

Approaching the summer home community of Potato Patch, you see a sign identifying the "Isabella Trail No. 67." It is named for Isabella "Brownie" Brown, who with her husband, Bud, are two of Arizona's greatest modern trailblazers. It's one of the few trails in Arizona named for a living person.

Three miles north of Potato Patch is Walker, on Lynx Creek, one of the sites where placer gold was discovered in 1863, leading to the founding of Prescott. The town was named for Captain Joseph Rutherford Walker, one of the West's greatest explorers and leader of the first gold seekers in this area. Today it is the setting for many summer homes.

The rest of our trip is an easy seven-mile drive on paved road past Hilltop Campground (39 campsites here) and Lynx Lake to the junction with State Route 69, four miles east of Prescott.

— *Marshall Trimble*

Desert Floral Wonderland

Desert scenery • Castle Creek • Lost treasure
Arizona's first resort • Lake Pleasant recreation

Back around the turn of the century, when the Rockefellers and Vanderbilts vacationed at Castle Hot Springs, they got off their private railway cars at Hot Springs Junction (today's Morristown), a dozen miles southeast of Wickenburg. They were fed and bedded down for the night at Frank Murphy's hotel, and next day they piled into a stagecoach for the 25-mile trip to Arizona's first resort.

Today, Murphy's hotel is divided in half by U.S. Route 60. One building, a private residence, sits on the southwest side; the other, the Morristown Grocery Store, is on the northeast. The proprietor is John Hardee, who has been here all his 77 years.

His grandfather, John Morgan Hardee, came to these parts in the 1880s and ranched at the JL Bar. He was also a Yavapai County deputy sheriff at the nearby mining camp of Briggs, now a ghost town. John Morgan Hardee's son Shade took a job in 1913 as a chauffeur, hauling tourists in a seven-passenger Cadillac from Hot Springs Junction to the resort.

At least one lost treasure story has its genesis near Morristown. It all began when a courier hauling two large gold bars was waylaid by a pair of bandits on the Hassayampa River. He killed both bandits in the ensuing melee, but was fatally wounded himself. He crawled up an arroyo, buried the gold bars at the foot of a large mesquite tree, and lived just long enough to tell his rescuers about it.

They searched in vain, never finding the gold. As far as anybody knows, those gold bars are still "somewhere out there."

Our back road trip begins on a road about a quarter mile east of the Morristown Grocery Store. It crosses State Route 74 and then becomes a dirt road that's rough in places. This terrain is high Sonoran Desert, a realm of wonderful diversity, with a predominance of green-bark palo verde trees, venerable creosote, and stately saguaro cactus. Mesquite thrives

(LEFT) *Stately saguaro cactuses thrive in the high Sonoran Desert along the road from Morristown to Lake Pleasant.* JAMES TALLON

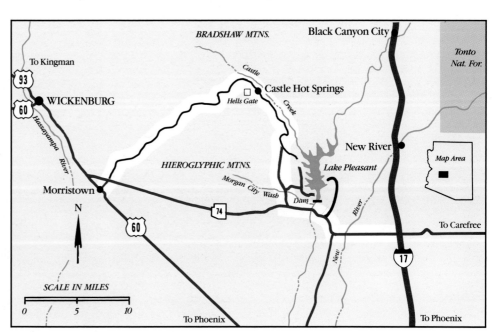

Best time to go
Spring; good all year

Degree of difficulty
Easy to moderate

Type of vehicle
High clearance vehicle preferred; sedan can make it

Travel time
Six hours

Road type
Dirt, rocky, shallow creeks

Elevation
1,500 - 2,500 feet

Terrain
Desert, mountain, foothills, canyons, lake

Features
High desert, exceptional spring wildflowers, history

along the banks of numerous desert washes, which flood dangerously in stormy weather.

The best time to travel this road is in the early spring (March-April), when the galaxy of desert wild flowers carpet the land with a profusion of variegated colors. The variety of Nature's own tapestry makes this one of the more scenic desert drives in the state.

The road passes north of the wild and rugged Hieroglyphic Mountains and winds its way around a rocky labyrinth of picturesque passes and small boulder-choked canyons. These mountains are mis-named because there are no hieroglyphics, but a profusion of petroglyphs (Indian carvings on rocks) may be found in the area. There's also abundant evidence of gold mining, past and present.

Nineteen miles from Morristown the road drops down into Castle Creek. Following the wash, the road leads through the JL Bar Ranch. Less than a mile east of the ranch is a turnoff to the right that goes up to a scenic viewpoint. Don't miss it! This site, once used by resort guests for picnics, overlooks Crater Canyon, a deep abyss of jagged rocks. Beyond it are Little Hell's Gate and Big Hell's Gate, two interesting geologic formations. Topographic maps, obtainable at map stores, will help you identify many such features on back road trips.

Just half a mile farther, you come upon the venerable resort of Castle Hot Springs. For many centuries, Indians who came to bathe in the healing waters were given safe passage, even during hostilities. Later pioneer burro drivers stopped here to soothe their aching bones in the hot mineral waters.

The first white men to see this beautiful green valley, in 1867, were U.S. Cavalry troops from Fort Whipple. Frank Murphy, the famed railroad and mining entrepreneur, acquired the property in 1896 and built Arizona's first major resort hotel here. Only 30 guests registered that first season, but its fame soon spread across the nation. Some 590 palm trees were planted on the property and a golf course was laid out.

Castle Hot Springs has not been operated as a resort since a fire destroyed the dining hall in 1976. It's off limits to visitors now, but you can see it from the road.

The road east of this palm-studded valley follows Castle Creek for a few miles and should be avoided in wet weather. It's eight miles from the former resort to the new highway leading into Lake Pleasant.

The lake, a beautiful blue jewel in the desert is a favorite with boaters, fishermen and other water sports enthusiasts. The new Waddell Dam holds 10,500 acre feet of water. A new visitors center presents a beautiful panoramic view of the lake and the spectacular surrounding desert.

(TOP AND CENTER LEFT) *Skirting the Hieroglyphic Mountains, the road dips and reels like a drunken cowhand on a three-legged horse.*

(LEFT) *Bring your camera and plenty of color film on this adventure through desert flora.*
PHOTOS BY WESLEY HOLDEN

(INSET) *Bright-hued strawberry hedgehog and brittlebush are two of this rocky land's floral offerings.*

(TOP RIGHT) *Hell's Gate Canyon offers some memorable overlooks and remarkable geologic formations.*

(RIGHT) *Arizona's first resort hotel, Castle Hot Springs, was a delightfully green oasis for many years. It opened before the turn of the century, but as of this printing it was closed for redevelopment.*
PHOTOS BY JAMES TALLON

ROAD IN RIVER BOTTOM NEXT 3 MILES DO NOT ATTEMPT TO CROSS WHEN FLOODED

From the turnoff into Lake Pleasant, it's just five miles back to State Route 74 and another 12 miles from there to Interstate 17 at the Carefree Highway.

While you're at the intersection of the Lake Pleasant road and State Route 74, you are but a short distance from the mislaid gold in Morgan City Wash. Back in 1934, hard times sent many a down-and-outer into these gold-laden hills to seek his fortune. The story is told that one Palmer C. Ashley did strike pay dirt in a nearby wash. But today nobody knows exactly where it was.

Some folks ask: Why, if I know so much about these lost treasures, don't I go out and find them for myself? As story-teller Oren Arnold used to say, "one finds more gold writing about lost mines than searching for them." And the man was right.

— *Marshall Trimble*

(TOP) *Lake Pleasant's azure waters paint an alluring picture. The lake offers endless hours of pleasure for sailors, power boaters, and fishing enthusiasts.*

(ABOVE) *California poppies blanket the desert in springtime.*

(RIGHT) *The end of a perfect day of sailing at Lake Pleasant.* PHOTOS BY JAMES TALLON

Storybook Pleasant Valley

A climb in the Sierra Anchas • Memories of a range war
Young • Cherry Creek Hill and the Mogollon Rim

Just 80 miles northeast of Phoenix, there is an area so isolated that it takes on an aura of dark mystery if you haven't been there — and becomes a pretty memory once you have.

Pleasant Valley is not served by pavement, except the short strip through the village of Young. Isolation has helped preserve the legends of the Pleasant Valley War, a bitter feud that centered in the valley a hundred years ago.

You probably could make the trip as far as Pleasant Valley most days in winter, but the adventure would be more enjoyable spring through fall.

It begins at a traffic light between Miami and Globe, 85 miles east of Phoenix. State Route 88 leaves U.S. Route 60 here and winds north along Pinal Creek. Thirteen miles out, it crosses some low mountains, and you are presented with a panoramic view of Roosevelt Lake.

(ABOVE) *Cross this Salt River bridge and head to the Sierra Anchas and Pleasant Valley.* WESLEY HOLDEN

(LEFT) *The majestic panorama of Roosevelt Lake with Four Peaks in the background on State Route 288 between the Globe-Miami area and the tiny community of Young.* JEFF KIDA

Best time to go	April through October
Degree of difficulty	Moderate
Type of vehicle	High clearance preferred
Travel time	Six hours; good camping for overnight
Road type	Dirt, some paving
Elevation	3,500 - 7,500 feet
Terrain	Desert, mountains, forest
Features	Scenery, history, fishing

It's another couple of miles to the junction with State Route 288, which departs to the right. The road is paved for the first 10 miles. It crosses the Salt River

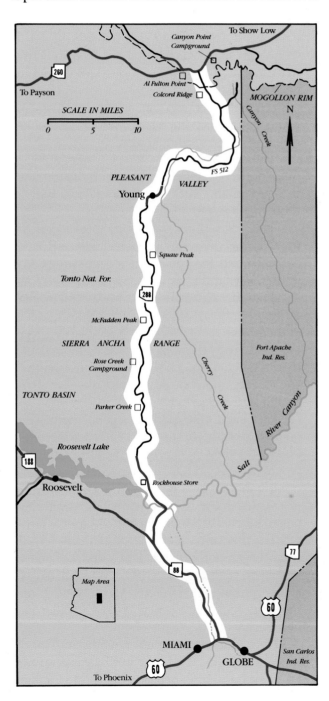

on a narrow bridge, and passes Rockhouse Store, the last commercial establishment until you reach Young.

As the pavement ends, you begin climbing the west face of the Sierra Ancha range — "Wide Mountains" in Spanish.

After about seven miles of winding narrow grades, you may want to turn off on a short road to the west (marked only by a stop sign) to a scenic overlook. The dramatic canyon cut into the red rock face of the Sierra Anchas and the view across Roosevelt Lake to Four Peaks is worth the side trip.

A sign warns you to watch for deer, and it means what it says. We slowed to a crawl for two whitetail does standing in the road.

Pull out when you can, and look below. As you climb, you gain an impressive view of the mountains receding to the south and west.

The entrance to Rose Creek Campground is 38 miles north of Globe. Just beyond is the entrance to the Workman Creek Recreation Area, with only those facilities provided by nature.

The road skirts 7,135-foot McFadden Peak, topped by a Forest Service lookout tower. Route 288 descends and the mountain top opens up: Lower, sparser vegetation lets you see where you're going.

There are 15 Squaw Peaks in Arizona (according to the U.S. Board of Geographic Names), and most of them were named for their resemblance to female breasts. Usually the comparison is no more flattering than the name "squaw," but 52 miles north of Globe you'll come upon one peak that looks — well, more than a little suggestive.

Fifty-eight miles north of Globe, there is a vista point to the right. Here you get your first view of Pleasant Valley, a storybook picture of tidy fields, groves of trees, and scattered dwellings.

It's another two miles to the valley, which was first settled in the 1870s. It was a long way from what passed for civilization in the rest of Arizona Territory.

The Pleasant Valley War, or Graham-Tewksbury Feud, began early in the 1880s and became most violent in the summer of 1887. While it ranged far across central and northern Arizona, the grimmest shootings took place here in Pleasant Valley and in nearby canyons.

Five years later, after neighboring ranchers thought they had ended the war by vigilante action, Ed Tewksbury ambushed and killed Tom Graham in Tempe. It was the final killing in the feud.

(ABOVE AND RIGHT) *The road to Young leads from the eastern shore of Roosevelt Lake to the Eden known as Pleasant Valley. Visitors and locals enjoy the rustic ambience of the appropriately named Antler Cafe in the quiet community of Young. Tewksbury and Graham Boulevards serve as reminders of the bloody Pleasant Valley War a century ago. Today, the valley lives up to its name, and families lead the good life on fertile farms and ranches.* PHOTOS BY JEFF KIDA

GRAHAM BLVD

PHOTOS BY
JEFF KIDA

(LEFT) *Binoculars help you see why they call this formation, located south of Young, Elephant Rock.*

(ABOVE) *Giant peach leaf willows dot the meadow along Canyon Creek.*

(BELOW) *Playful Canyon Creek romps through the rocks. The fishing is great, but you may just want to stop and wade a bit.* PHOTOS BY WESLEY HOLDEN

(RIGHT) *Sunset's glow enhances the vista from the Mogollon Rim, near Al Fulton Point, the end of this back road trip.* JEFF KIDA

Zane Grey immortalized the Pleasant Valley War in his novel, *To the Last Man*. But the most thorough account yet written of that grim conflict is *A Little War of Our Own*, by former *Arizona Highways* editor Don Dedera, published in 1987.

Pleasant Valley is peaceful now, and the people are friendly. There are apple orchards here, and windmills feed pretty ponds. Services are rudimentary, but there are cafes, gas stations, and stores. Check the gas gauge, because it's a long way to the next town.

State Route 288 takes a 90-degree turn to the east for a mile or so. Much of the frontage property is pasture; old barns and corn cribs give the landscape a lived-in look. The cemetery, where some victims of the Pleasant Valley War are buried, is on a little rise north of the road.

Then the road turns north along Cherry Creek. The pavement ends, and the road begins climbing Cherry Creek Hill. State Route 288 ends just north of Young, and the road becomes Forest Road 512 of the Tonto National Forest. You'll find the road is well maintained and relatively smooth.

Where Forest Road 512 reaches its first summit and levels out for a while, we saw a flock of wild turkeys. There also are several groves of taller than usual Gambel's oak trees among the pines. Young is at 5,184 feet elevation, and the road will climb to 7,550 feet on the Mogollon Rim.

It takes a while to get there.

The road meanders, running along ridgetops and re-crossing Cherry Creek where it is only a shallow dry wash. Two roads to the right (east) lead to Canyon Creek, a stream revered by trout fishermen. Tonto National Forest has several primitive camping areas near Canyon Creek, but there is no potable water.

The road approaches the Mogollon Rim along the crest of Colcord Ridge, so you don't have to climb a winding grade as you would farther west. (You have already climbed your grade back on Cherry Creek Hill.) The Rim's usual parapet is to the left, just before 7,513-foot Colcord Mountain obscures it from view.

The road is on relatively level ground as it joins paved State Route 260, 25 miles north of Young. Turn left to go to Kohl's Ranch and Payson, and turn right to Heber and Show Low.

Once you have been to Pleasant Valley — many Arizona natives still have not — you may have a better understanding of the Pleasant Valley War. But it's likely that you'll always remember the trip for more pleasant reasons.
— *James E. Cook*

Blue River Wilderness

White Mountain getaway • Lush Lee Valley • Mt. Baldy hiking trail
Crescent and Big lakes • Hunting, fishing, skiing, sight-seeing

Leaving Arizona's major cities for a visit to the countryside of the White Mountains is a little like descending into a funnel. You start on a paved highway among modern buildings and corporate headquarters, wind your way down to narrower paving through a mighty canyon, and eventually you're on a dirt road 200 miles from the bustle of the city. The calendar seems to shed more than a hundred years.

Begin this excursion to the scenic mountain paradise between Sunrise and the Blue River by driving to Globe, about two hours from either Phoenix or Tucson.

It's another two hours from Globe to Sunrise via Show Low on U.S. Route 60 and State Route 260, but the scenery along the drive changes so dramatically that the time will seem much shorter. Thirty-five miles north of Globe, you'll drive through spectacular Salt River Canyon, a miniature version of the Grand Canyon. Another hour's drive brings you to Show Low, gateway to the White Mountain vacationland. There you leave U.S. Route 60 and take scenic State Route 260 southeast through the communities of Lakeside, Pinetop, and McNary.

Sunrise, 32 miles east of McNary, is a resort motel on the Fort Apache Indian Reservation. In summer, the 9,200-foot elevation guarantees comfortable days, and the nights are cool enough for a sweater. In winter, the Sunrise ski slopes come alive. There are 11 lifts to

(TOP) *White Mountain Apache cowboys herd their cattle in time-honored fashion along the road to the Blue River country.*

(LEFT) *You'll find few spots on this earth with more serene beauty than on the banks of the Blue River in the vast White Mountain wilderness.*
PHOTOS BY PETER ENSENBERGER

carry skiers up to the 700 acres of ski terrain that flanks the 11,000-foot crest of Apache Peak. Sunrise, four miles south of State Route 260 on State Route 273, faces aspen- and spruce-covered hills dotted with 25 lakes and numerous streams where fishing is good.

Now we leave the paving and begin our green wilderness adventure.

A few miles south of Sunrise, the graded dirt road crosses the west fork of the Little Colorado River.

Best time to go	May through October
Degree of difficulty	Moderate
Type of vehicle	High clearance preferred
Travel time	Six hours; good camping for overnight
Road type	Dirt, some paving
Elevation	5,600 - 9,200 feet
Terrain	Desert, mountains, forest
Features	Scenery, hiking, history

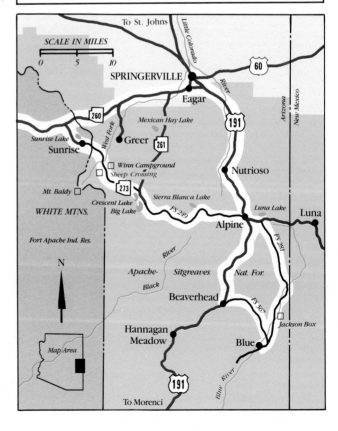

At the river, a spur to the right leads to the parking lot at Sheep Crossing, so named because it's part of a sheep trail that connected the White Mountain summer pastures to the winter pastures and markets at Phoenix.

Here you may want to leave your car and hike the trail up Mt. Baldy, elevation 11,590 feet. In the spring the meadow is filled with wildflowers; in the fall it is flecked with the golden leaves blown from quaking aspens. The trail switchbacks through dense forest and eventually climbs above the trees onto the broad and sparsely covered upper slope of one of Arizona's tallest mountains.

The road from Sheep Crossing drops into the wide and verdant Lee Valley Recreation Area after crossing the West Fork. Winn Campground soon comes up on your left, with 63 spaces, easy pullouts, restrooms, and water. There is a fee for camping and picknicking.

The graded road winds from Winn to Crescent Lake, and suddenly you're on pavement again, driving along the eastern side of Big Lake. Take Forest Road 115 from the paved road to reach the lake's campgrounds, gas station, and boat rental area. It's only two miles from the pavement to the store and gas pump.

After leaving Big Lake, the pavement ends as abruptly as it began. The graded Forest Road 249 is usually smooth and well-maintained, and there are several wide spots to stop and watch for the elk and deer that are plentiful throughout the area. Between Big Lake and Alpine, the elevation drops from 9,000 feet to 8,046 feet in about 20 miles.

(LEFT) *Where could life be better than at Big Lake on a summer morning? Arizona's premier trout lake, the 500-acre impoundment offers rental boats, boat ramps, fish cleaning stations, a well-stocked store, and ample campsites.* DAVID ELMS

INSETS: (TOP LEFT) *Sierra Blanca Lake.*
(BOTTOM LEFT) *Mexican Hay Lake.*
PHOTOS BY PETER ENSENBERGER
(INSET, RIGHT) *Crescent Lake.* JACK DYKINGA
All grace the White Mountains in eastern Arizona. When you visit, bring blankets and warm clothing — it's chilly up there at 9,000 feet.

(FOLLOWING PANEL) *The lure of spring flowers or fall leaves attracts many hikers to the trail up Mt. Baldy (11,590 feet), a sacred mountain of the Apache Indians. The summit is closed to non-Indians.* DAVID ELMS

Alpine is a tiny community with two motels, a few small stores and restaurants, and two churches, one Catholic and one Protestant. It's all but deserted in wintertime, although the area offers some of the best cross-country skiing terrain in the state. In summer its population swells with visitors from Arizona's and New Mexico's desert cities.

Alpine is at the center of all major access routes to both the Blue and Black rivers.

The Blue River, which meanders gracefully in a deep canyon along the Arizona-New Mexico border, leads to a community called Blue. To reach it, follow U.S. Route 180 four miles east of Alpine. Just before Luna Lake, take Forest Road 281 on the right.

This route, which is well-maintained because it is used by local mail carriers, reaches Upper Blue Campground after 13.3 miles. A second campground is located six miles farther at the junction with FR 567. Prehistoric rock art can be found on boulders within the campground. The road is narrow and the two campgrounds on the river are small, so trailers and motor homes are not encouraged.

Along the Blue River, between the campgrounds, the road crosses several small bridges and swings through Jackson Box, an area of vertical red cliffs and giant cottonwood trees. The river bottom is paved at the crossing, and water is rarely high enough to cause any problems, even for a passenger car.

The "community" of Blue actually consists of widely-scattered ranches, a stone building that was once the post office, and a one-room schoolhouse. Much of the surrounding area is part of the Apache-Sitgreaves National Forest.

If you want to get away from it all, this remote, beautiful country is the answer. Alpine, 24 miles north, is the nearest town. Morenci, 80 miles to the south, and Reserve, New Mexico, 30 miles east, are the closest towns in their respective directions. With a good pair of wings, if you headed directly west of Blue, you wouldn't hit anything resembling a town until you reached the outskirts of Phoenix.

Don't look for restaurants, stores, or gas stations along the Blue River.

As far as anyone knows, the Blue River country was unpopulated by white men until the 1880s when homesteads were established by Joseph H. Toles Cosper, Fred Fritz, Sr., and Henry Jones, cattlemen from Texas and New Mexico. Also on the Blue River they found sanctuary from the likes of Billy the Kid, who was exercising his trigger finger in New Mexico.

But they encountered new dangers in a large population of black and grizzly bears. The last known grizzly in the Blue River area was killed in 1935. The black bears are still out there, but are rarely a threat to hikers.

To return, retrace your drive back to Alpine.

WATCH FOR ANIMALS

Or, for a change of scenery, return to Alpine via Forest Road 567. It winds 12 miles up the spine of a long steep ridge to State Route 191. From there it's 14 miles north to Alpine. From Alpine, go north via Nutrioso to Springerville, and then west to Sunrise on State Route 260.

This Sunrise-to-Blue loop drive is only 140 miles round-trip, but allow a full day for it. The abundant wildlife and picture postcard landscapes will entice you to stop frequently.   — Sam Negri

Peaceful and beautiful, the forests of the White Mountain and Blue River country renew the spirit and provide a home for a wide variety of wildlife.

(TOP LEFT) *View from Forest Road 567 in the Blue River country.* DAVID ELMS

(ABOVE) *Rocky mountain mule deer graze in a pine-covered meadow.* PETER ENSENBERGER

(TOP RIGHT) *The small (three campsites) but inviting Upper Blue Campground, 13 miles south of Alpine.* W. RANDALL IRVINE

(CENTER RIGHT) *A chipmunk family chatters a friendly greeting.* ELIZABETH ELMS

(RIGHT) *For years a rare sight in Arizona , the elusive wild turkey is making a comeback.* PETER ENSENBERGER

Tour 13: 50 Miles, Starts from Apache Junction

Apache Trail

Some of the old-time Arizonans, who traveled the Apache Trail out of necessity early in this century, have never wanted to repeat the experience. They added to the road's dark reputation, and the tales of terror on Fish Creek Hill.

Too bad. While the Apache Trail is still a monument to primitive engineering, safe modern vehicles now permit leisurely sightseeing through unspoiled desert.

State Route 88 reaches three large fishing and boating lakes in the mountains northeast of Phoenix. It explores a region of lush desert, and goes deep into Arizona history and legend.

A thousand years ago, prehistoric Salado Indians used a foot trail along the canyons of the Salt River and its tributaries. Known later as the Tonto Trail, it was commonly used in the 19th century by Indian traders or raiders, and by white settlers.

Pioneers in the Phoenix area realized late in the 1800s that their prosperity depended on building a reservoir to store and regulate water in the Salt River. So Roosevelt Dam was built (1905-'11) where Tonto Creek joins the Salt.

A road was built along the old trail to carry men and material to the dam site, traveled first by wagons and stagecoaches, and later by trucks and automobiles. Former President Theodore Roosevelt rode to the dedication of the dam in a Kissell Kar in 1911, a trip that took six hours. For a time, this was the main road into Phoenix from north and east.

(ABOVE, LEFT) *The legend of the Lost Dutchman Mine, still undiscovered after many decades, is commemorated by this monument at Apache Junction.*

(FAR LEFT) *The Superstition Mountains brood moodily over the campground at Lost Dutchman State Park as you begin this journey along the Apache Trail.*
PHOTOS BY JAMES TALLON

Best time to go
October through May

Degree of difficulty
Easy to moderate

Type of vehicle
Family car

Travel time
Six hours

Road type
Dirt, some paving

Elevation
2,000 - 3,500 feet

Terrain
Desert, mountain foothills

Features
Mining camps, spring wildflowers, beautiful lake vistas, Indian ruins

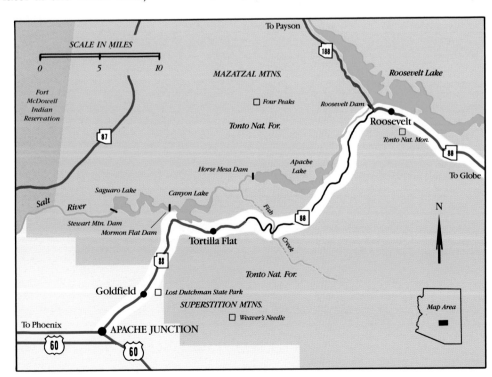

(ABOVE INSET) *The one-lane bridge at the bottom of Fish Creek Hill.*

(LEFT) *Aerial view of the Apache Trail's tortuous route down Fish Creek Hill. Originally built as the supply road for the construction of Roosevelt Dam, the Trail and the desert scenery it traverses have inspired generations of motorists. President Theodore Roosevelt, after his journey to dedicate the dam named for him, described the road as "one of the most spectacular best-worth-seeing sights of the world."* PHOTOS BY JAMES TALLON

(LEFT INSET) *Canyon Lake, formed by Mormon Flat Dam on the Salt River, features a marina, coffee shop, and a 1 1/2-hour lake cruise aboard the 52-foot paddlewheeler* Dolly. JERRY JACKA

The Forest Service has designated the Apache Trail a National Scenic Byway, and the Arizona State Transportation Board chose it to be the state's first Historic Road. You can travel it year-round. In summer, carry drinking water and watch for flash floods.

State Route 88 leaves U.S. Route 60 at Apache Junction, east of Phoenix. Immediately you're into legend, for the road runs around the northwest base of the Superstition Mountains supposed site of the Lost Dutchman Mine.

In 1892, gold was discovered for sure at Goldfield, 4.5 miles northeast of Apache Junction. Goldfield was a ghost town for most of this century, but it has since been revived as a visitor attraction, offering a restaurant, saloon, and mine tours.

Half a mile farther is the entrance to Lost Dutchman State Park. This 300-acre park has 35 rudimentary campsites, 15 picnic ramadas, and a native plant trail. Fine stands of saguaro cactus line the Apache Trail, rising above the thicker mesquite, paloverde, ironwood, cholla, and prickly pear. Whip-like branches of the ocotillo wave gently from the edge of the road, as does the occasional century plant.

Weaver's Needle Vista is seven miles from Apache Junction. The top of the stone spire appears through a notch in the Superstitions. Jacob Waltz, the old Dutchman who died without telling anyone where his fabled Lost Dutchman Mine was located, said it was in the shadow of the needle.

You'll see 7,645-foot Four Peaks to the northeast as the Apache Trail begins to twist like a snake with appendicitis, climbing ridges, making hairpin turns, and plunging into new drainages. Signs warn that vehicles should not exceed 30 feet in length.

Although the road is paved, the posted speed limit is 25, and even that is frequently optimistic. It's not a place to hurry, even when you know the bass are waiting in Canyon or Apache lakes, which can be reached only by the Apache Trail. The road touches Canyon Lake at several points, giving access to boat ramps. Tonto National Forest provides some 80 campsites and 60 picnic sites.

Two miles beyond Canyon Lake is Tortilla Flat, a small community with a tourist store, historic memorabilia, and nearby 77-unit campground. The pavement ends at milepost 22, five meandering miles past Tortilla Flat. From there on, the road is a bit washboarded, but well-maintained.

(ABOVE) *Today the Apache Trail offers views pioneers never saw, such as water skiing on Canyon Lake.*

(RIGHT) *Farther down the road to the east is Apache Lake, filling a rugged desert canyon.*

(INSET) *You can camp on the shore of Apache Lake and launch your boat after breakfast in the brisk morning air.* PHOTOS BY JAMES TALLON

(TOP) *A thousand years ago the Salado Indians occupied the cliff dwelling now known as Tonto National Monument, four miles southeast of Roosevelt Dam.*

(ABOVE) *Visitors may climb up to the Tonto ruins and see for themselves what life was like there so long ago.*

(LEFT) *This is the view the ancient inhabitants had, without the lake of course, from their Tonto cliff home.*
PHOTOS BY JAMES TALLON

(TOP RIGHT) *Theodore Roosevelt Dam, completed in 1911, tamed the capricious Salt River and made possible the system of lakes and canals that enabled Phoenix to become one of the largest desert cities in the world.*
WESLEY HOLDEN

A couple of miles beyond the end of the pavement, the road plunges off notorious Fish Creek Hill into Fish Creek Canyon. Fortunately, when you attack the two-mile grade from west to east you are going downhill and hugging the bluff. Uphill traffic is on the cliff's edge and a bit more scary.

Downhill was not the preferred direction in stagecoach days. Coaches carrying passengers to Roosevelt Dam stopped at the top of the grade, it is said, while the driver fired three signal shots. A teamster then came up from the bottom of the hill and hitched a mule team to the rear of the stage, facing toward Phoenix. Walking backward, the mules braked the stage on its steepest descent. Prudent passengers often walked to the bottom.

It is four miles on to Apache Lake Vista, the first of several spectacular views of this long, narrow lake. A road from the vista leads to a marina and three dozen campsites. Apache Lake continues to appear for another 10 miles.

Suddenly the road pops out on an open shelf carved from the stone cliff, and you get a full-face view of Roosevelt Dam. Built of blocks of native stone, it is the world's largest masonry arch dam.

There are viewpoints to look over the dam and the blue expanse of Roosevelt Lake, which is popular with fishermen, boaters, and water skiers. Few come via Fish Creek Hill, however; they prefer to take U.S. Route 60 to Globe and travel the paved State Route 88 from there to Roosevelt.

Four miles southeast of the dam, toward Globe, Tonto National Monument offers a glimpse at the culture of the vanished Salado people, who lived in cliff dwellings from A.D. 900 to 1400.

For variety, return to Apache Junction and Phoenix via the well-traveled Globe highway to complete a day's drive of memorable beauty and historical significance.

— *James E. Cook*

Pinal Pioneer Parkway

Historic Florence • Flowering desert • Oracle • Abandoned mining camps
Gila and San Pedro rivers • Winkelman, Kearny, and Superior

This trip along one of Arizona's "blue highways" (secondary but paved) offers a rich variety of experiences ranging from the spectacular Sonoran Desert and an open-pit copper mine to historic territorial towns.

We start at Florence Junction, 48 miles east of Phoenix on U.S. Route 60, go south to Oracle Junction, and then return to Florence Junction via Hayden and Superior.

The first 16 miles to the historic town of Florence along State Route 79, is especially beautiful in the spring when flowers bloom profusely.

You're really missing something special if you don't leave the highway and drive down the main street of Florence. It's one of the best kept main streets in Arizona, and it looks like a movie set for a southwestern town (*Murphy's Romance*, starring James Garner and Sally Field, was filmed here).

In Florence you'll want to visit McFarland State Park and see the Victorian-era courthouse. That courthouse, built in 1891 at a cost of $29,999, still is in use. The only thing not working in the building is the clock in the tower, which was never installed because funds ran out. So a fake clock face shows the time in Florence eternally at nine o'clock.

Now it's time to drive down the Pinal Pioneer Parkway, 42 miles southeast to Oracle Junction. The parkway was established in 1961 by the

Arizona Highway Department as a scenic desert preserve uncluttered by billboards or other man-made obstructions. The elevation runs from 1,500 feet at Florence to 3,300 feet at the southern end.

Following the gentle rains of winter, the desert comes alive in the spring and late summer with a profusion of wildflowers.

This is the higher elevation of the Sonoran Desert, the most prolific of all the world's deserts.

Best time to go	October through May
Degree of difficulty	Easy
Type of vehicle	Family car
Travel time	Six hours
Road type	Paved
Elevation	1,500 -3,500 feet
Terrain	Desert, foothills
Features	Spring and summer wildflowers, historic mining towns

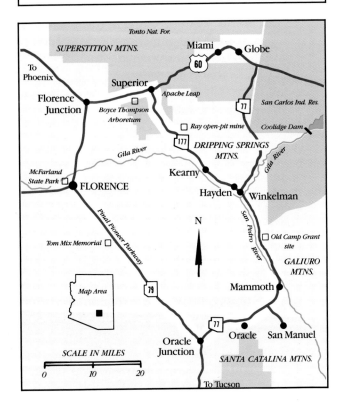

(ABOVE) *Tom Mix, the famous cowboy film star, is remembered with this monument south of Florence, where he died in a 1940 automobile accident.*

(LEFT) *You never leave the pavement on this Pinal County outing, but you see desert wilderness far from the city lights. This view is along the road from Kearny to Superior.* PHOTOS BY JAMES TALLON

Drought-resistant plants such as prickly pear, cholla, yucca, catclaw, mesquite, and the stately saguaro luxuriate here.

The land around Pinal Pioneer Parkway is a bird-watchers paradise. Hawks, vultures, Gila woodpeckers, white wing doves, and the ubiquitous roadrunner are in abundance.

Several roadside rest areas with ramadas, grills, tables, and benches are provided. One is the Tom Mix memorial, where the famed cowboy movie star met his death in a 1940 auto accident. You may want to stop for a picnic lunch along the parkway.

At Oracle Junction, turn east on State Route 77 toward Oracle and Mammoth. "Curly Bill" Neal and his wife Ann, two of the most successful and enterprising African Americans in Arizona history built a famous health resort at Oracle in 1895.

Located at the northeast end of the beautiful Santa Catalina Mountains, Oracle has been a favorite tourist attraction ever since. Here the oaks and granite dells give way to the grassy slopes that angle toward the San Pedro River, which can be seen from here as a thin green line through the knobby bluffs that flank the stream. Off to the east are the lofty Galiuro Mountains, one of the finest and most rugged wilderness areas in the nation.

Seven miles east of Oracle is the junction leading to the "new" copper town of San Manuel, established in 1954. And five miles northeast of the junction is the town of Mammoth, which took its name from the mammoth ore body discovered two miles west of here in 1872. The copper ore was shipped down the mountain to the mill in huge buckets hung from a tramway, and the buckets were filled on the return trip with water for thirsty miners.

Eight miles northwest of Mammoth, driving along the banks of the San Pedro River, you'll cross Aravaipa Creek. A short drive down Aravaipa Road (turn right just north of the creek) will take you to several shady spots to picnic or cool your feet in the waters of the San Pedro.

(OPPOSITE, CLOCKWISE FROM TOP LEFT)
This sign marks the Pinal Pioneer Parkway, State Route 79 near Florence, where desert flora and fauna abound. The Pinal County Courthouse in Florence, with its clock perpetually set at 9:00. Downtown Florence, where the movie Murphy's Romance was filmed is being lovingly restored by local citizens. McFarland State Historic Park, named for Ernest W. McFarland, former Arizona governor, state supreme court justice, and U.S. Senator is a museum containing turn-of-the-century memorabilia.

(CLOCKWISE FROM ABOVE) *Pinal Pioneer Parkway spreads a tempting feast for the nature lover. For the visitor or newcomer to Arizona, roadside signs identify plants like the bright green paloverde tree, staghorn cholla cactus flowers, chain fruit chollas amid brittlebush, and the saguaro upon whose fruit a white wing dove feasts.* PHOTOS BY JAMES TALLON

Old-timers used to tell of the notorious drink called the "San Pedro Torpedo," made with tequila, whiskey, wood alcohol, a plug of tobacco, and the head of a rattlesnake. The concoction was considered mild until you added the final ingredient, a shot glass of water from the San Pedro River. That was the kicker guaranteed to make the incautious imbiber see double and feel single.

Historic Old Camp Grant was located here on Aravaipa Creek in 1860-71. In the bloody Camp Grant Massacre of 1871, angry Tucson vigilantes raided an Aravaipa Apache village near the army post and killed a hundred Indians, most of them women and children.

Eleven miles farther on State Route 77 are the twin towns of Winkelman and Hayden. This fertile valley at the junction of the Gila and San Pedro rivers has a rich history. Sobaipuri Indians, a Pima people, were living here when Father Eusebio Kino passed through in 1697. Anglos started farming operations here in the 1870's.

You leave State Route 77 at Winkelman and take State Route 177 nine miles northwest to Kearny, a community built in 1958 by the Kennecott Copper Company. It's on the Gila River, where mountain men such as Ewing Young, Kit Carson, and James Ohio Pattie trapped beaver in the 1820s. In 1846, General Stephen Watts Kearny, for whom the town is named, led a hundred U.S. dragoons along the Gila to invade California during the war with Mexico.

Six miles beyond Kearny are two once-roaring territorial towns, Kelvin and Riverside, on opposite banks of the Gila a couple of miles south of the highway. You'll see the Dripping Springs Mountains off to the right. This rugged range was rich in minerals and made a hefty contribution to early Arizona's mining industry.

Now you are in Copper Canyon, where once stood the communities of Ray and Sonora. Some 30 years ago, these towns were packed up and moved a few miles down the road to the new community of Kearny. On their former site is the open-pit Ray Mine, a spectacular sight worth a short detour to see.

Continuing northwest on State Route 177 for another 11 miles, you reach the lively copper town of Superior, nestled at the foot of the sheer Apache Leap.

Turn west on U.S. Highway 60 at Superior (you may want to stop by the Boyce Thompson Arboretum on the way) for 15 miles to Florence Junction and the end of our loop trip. — *Marshall Trimble*

(TOP LEFT) *Hayden, on the return portion of the tour, is a sprightly copper mining community.*

(BOTTOM LEFT) *The Gila River, near Kearny, dons a brilliant wardrobe of fall finery.*

(CENTER) *An old-time ore train locomotive at Kearny is a reminder of the mining heritage of this Pinal County district.* PHOTOS BY JAMES TALLON

(RIGHT) *Historic Superior, a leading Arizona copper town, nestles at the foot of towering Apache Leap.*

(BELOW) *It's a man-made canyon, this open-pit Ray Mine, a scenic expanse on the site where the towns of Ray and Sonora once thrived.*
PHOTOS BY WESLEY HOLDEN

Colorado River Wildlife

**Yuma's historic port • Laguna and Imperial dams • Martinez Lake
Herons, geese, swans, and pelicans • Imperial National Wildlife Refuge**

A drive from Yuma to the Imperial National Wildlife Refuge will take you through a serene and exotic landscape where sea birds meet their cousins of the desert.

Yuma, a burgeoning city surrounded by corrugated volcanic mountains, thrives in the middle of one of America's hottest deserts. Running through this terrain, where winter temperatures are usually in the 70s, is Arizona's largest river, on which steamboat traffic was once a dominant feature.

Yes, Yuma was for several decades a busy port.

A river coursing through a desert seems strange enough. Add to this picture pelicans, gulls, and terns wafting overhead and blue herons standing near the marshy shores, and you begin to wonder if something peculiar hasn't happened to the earth's biosphere.

Salt water seems a long way off, but it's closer than it seems. The Colorado River, fattened a bit by the Gila River which joins it a little east of Yuma, bends westward through Yuma before plunging south to Mexico and the Sea of Cortez (also known as the Gulf of California), just a hundred road miles to the south. The birds, however, tend to do just what this tour does: follow the meandering river.

Before the construction of a series of dams, beginning with Laguna Dam in 1909, the river channel had a history of frequently reshaping its route, depending on the extent of floods. But today the Colorado is a tamed giant, and you can drive

(ABOVE) *One of the world's most sophisticated irrigation systems has turned the Yuma desert into a cornucopia of vegetables and fruits. Here lettuce workers harvest a crop of green gold.*

(LEFT) *On the Colorado River north of Yuma, waterfowl of many varieties find rest and refreshment at the Imperial National Wildlife Refuge.* PHOTOS BY JAMES TALLON

the levee road along its banks and camp along its reedy shores without trepidation.

This 68-mile roundtrip loop easily can be completed in a half a day. But we recommend you bring your camera, binoculars, and a picnic lunch and plan to spend the day.

Begin the tour at the junction of Interstate 8 and 16th Street in Yuma. Head east on 16th Street 5.5 miles to Laguna Dam Road, (Country Route 7E), turn left (a convenience store is on the northwest corner).

Best time to go	October through April
Degree of difficulty	Easy
Type of vehicle	Family car
Travel time	Five hours
Road type	Dirt, some paving
Elevation	100 - 500 feet
Terrain	Desert, river lakes
Features	Exceptional birdwatching, hiking, fishing

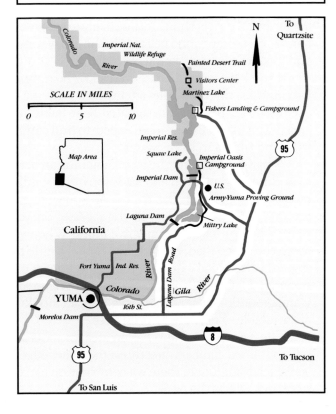

The flat paved road winds through irrigated vegetable farms for just under nine miles and then becomes a graded dirt road as it approaches Laguna Dam. You can drive this road with just about any vehicle, including a mobile home, but it's a little bumpy in some spots.

As you reach the dirt portion of the road, remember that the river is to your left and you always want to remain on the road closest to the river. Don't take any of the dirt roads you may see meandering off to the right.

Less than a mile after you begin the dirt road, you will begin to encounter camper pullouts on your left, flat against the river shore. You are likely to see grebes, herons, cormorants, and pelicans in the glassy waters, and Cooper's hawks soaring overhead.

If you have a small boat, even a row boat, bring it along. Less than two miles after you start driving on the dirt road, there is a designated boat launching area. If you like to fish, you can expect to find catfish, bass, and tilapia in these waters.

A half-mile beyond the boat launching area, the road climbs a gentle hill and leads you into a wildlife revegetation project. The river is on your left, and tranquil little lakes appear in the recesses on your right. The dirt road lasts only five miles. When you reach the paved road, turn left and in half a mile the Imperial Oasis road will be on your right. It leads past Imperial Dam, built in 1937, to Imperial Oasis Campground, where 256 spaces and all hookups are available. There are 31 campsites.

The campground also has an area for tents and self-contained campers directly on the river's edge. If you're ready for lunch, there is a combination grocery store and cafe at the oasis.

(CLOCKWISE FROM ABOVE) *U.S. Army tanks and artillery pieces are tested under desert conditions at the Yuma Proving Ground.* WESLEY HOLDEN

An unhurried trip on the so-called "levee road" along the Colorado River offers scenery and an abundance of wildlife found in few other places.

You can bring your small boat on this tour. Launch ramps are available at Imperial Oasis, Martinez Lake, and other locations along the river.

(OPPOSITE, TOP) *Camping along the river's edge offers an opportunity to observe varieties of wildlife.*

(RIGHT) *Sunset on the Colorado signals the end of another perfect day for these boaters.*
PHOTOS BY JAMES TALLON

(RIGHT) *The tower at Imperial wildlife refuge gives bird-watchers a birds-eye view of the many species that congregate here.*

(BELOW) *The Colorado, Arizona's largest river, has passed mighty dams and the Grand Canyon on its long and turbulent journey toward the Gulf of California.*

(OPPOSITE, CLOCKWISE FROM TOP) *Sunset's golden light paints a delightful picture of pintail ducks flushed from the river surface. A common egret searches for its supper at day's end. Mallards ride the gentle swells of the river. Pelicans, and a killdeer are two more denizens of this river country.*

PHOTOS BY JAMES TALLON

(RIGHT)
*Just having fun.
Hikers take
a self-portrait
while making
comical patterns
with their shadows.*
WESLEY HOLDEN

(CLOCKWISE FROM LEFT) *The family car easily travels
the road past a big horn sheep rock formation.
Views of the river valley await hikers on the one-mile
long Painted Desert Trail at Imperial National Wildlife
Refuge where interpretive trail markers provide
information about the sights.*
PHOTOS BY JAMES TALLON

When you leave the oasis and return to the main road, turn left, pass the U.S. Army's Yuma Proving Ground (where tanks and heavy vehicles are tested), and continue to the junction of U.S. Route 95. It's a little more than six miles southeast from Imperial Oasis cutoff to that junction.

Turn left onto U.S. Route 95 and drive approximately three miles to the cutoff on your left for Martinez Lake and Imperial National Wildlife Refuge. There is a sign on the highway directing you to the refuge. It's 10 miles from U.S. Route 95 on a paved road to the cutoff for the wildlife refuge, and three miles more on a dirt road from the cutoff to the visitor center.

Desert and river come together at the wildlife refuge, which was established in 1941 to protect the diverse plant and animal life that inhabit both ecosystems. You cannot camp at the refuge, but you can launch your boat in the translucent backwater lakes, fish, or simply sit and listen to the slap of the herons' feet as they run across the glassy surface.

There are four lookout points in the refuge, spaced roughly a mile apart. Stop at any of these points and look around; you'll see a remarkable contrast. The Sonoran Desert, one of the hottest and driest in the United States, fills the distance, but below you at any of the viewpoints is clear lake water surrounded by willows and a reedy fastness where migratory fowl are abundant.

Along the 30-mile stretch of the wildlife refuge, you may see Canada geese, golden and bald eagles, whistling swans, or black-crowned night herons. This may be your only opportunity to see the rare black rail and Yuma clapper rail. A bird list is available at the visitor center.

The refuge also contains a mile-long, self-guided interpretive trail. Known as the Painted Desert Trail, it begins a little less than three miles beyond the refuge headquarters and meanders through dramatic buff- and rust-colored boulders and craggy cliffs, leading eventually to a lookout that provides an impressive view of the river valley.

When you return to the paved road where you entered the refuge, the resort community of Martinez Lake is a half-mile to your right. Food and accommodations are available there. You can be back in Yuma, via U.S. Route 95, in 45 minutes. — *Sam Negri*

Swift Trail up Mount Graham

Mountain campgrounds • Riggs Lake
Trout fishing • Lots of wildlife, including bears

Swift Trail, the road that leads to the cool, green forests of the Pinaleno Mountains near Safford, will get you higher than any other road in southeastern Arizona.

For centuries, the range has provided desert dwellers with a refreshing respite from the summer heat; in fall it is a haven in which to experience the crisp air and golden foliage usually associated with more northern climate zones.

The Pinalenos are often referred to locally as "the Grahams" because of the prominence of the range's highest peak, Mt. Graham (also called High Peak), which pokes the clouds at a towering 10,717 feet above sea level. The road up the mountain goes only to 9,300 feet, but numerous hiking trails go higher.

Evidence of occupation by prehistoric peoples, whose shadowy footsteps you may be following, have been found at the base of the mountain around 3,000 feet, and amid the pines and aspens near Mt. Graham.

A 1907 map shows there were once seven sawmills on the mountain, although now there are none. One of the mills on Ash Creek had a flume (wooden chute) to lower timber from 9,000 feet to the 4,000-foot level, just above the town of Pima.

Spring and summer, when the hillsides are bright with red and lavender flowers have customarily been the liveliest on the mountain. Families that farmed along the Gila River near Pima, Thatcher, Safford, and Solomon herded their livestock and hauled their personal belongings up

the mountain as soon as it became too warm in the valley.

Shortly before the turn of the century, the Cluff brothers completed a wagon road up the north side of the mountain and charged people about a dollar per wagon to use it. Today's visitors need not be concerned about tolls; in 1935 the U.S. Forest Service built a road up the eastern side of the mountain from the junction of U.S. Route 191 and Swift Trail.

Best time to go	June through October
Degree of difficulty	Easy to moderate
Type of vehicle	Family car. **Caution:** steep winding road may cause vehicles to overheat
Travel time	Eight hours
Road type	Paved, some dirt
Elevation	3,000 - 10,028 feet
Terrain	Mountain
Features	Scenery, fishing, hiking, summer wildflowers

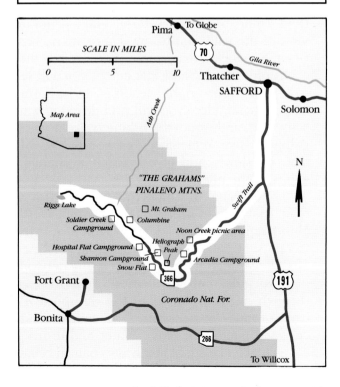

(LEFT) *How could anyone resist the allure of the scenic Pinaleno Mountains, locally known as the Grahams. The Swift Trail up Mount Graham climbs to altitudes of more than 9,000 feet, and 10,000 feet at Heliograph Peak.* DAVID ELMS

The Swift Trail cutoff leaves U.S. Route 191 about nine miles south of Safford. From the junction, it is 36 miles on to Riggs Lake, the major feature at the top of the mountain.

The road is paved at the beginning, but 29 miles up the mountain, in the vicinity of Hospital Flat Campground, it turns to graded dirt. The road has many hairpin curves and the Forest Service prohibits trailers longer than 22 feet. However, the dirt portion is easily handled with a two-wheel-drive vehicle.

You will not find restaurants, gas stations, or overnight accommodations (other than campgrounds) on the mountain, although nearby Safford, with a population of about 7,500, has all these and medical services too.

As you start your drive up the mountain, you will first come to the Noon Creek picnic area, eight miles above the junction with U.S. Route 191. Drinking water, picnic tables, plenty of shade, and restrooms are available in this small grove of juniper and oak trees. Arcadia, the lowest campground, is four miles beyond Noon Creek at an altitude of 6,700 feet. There are 28 campsites, outhouses, drinking water, and tall ponderosa pines here.

Nine miles above Arcadia, note the sign on the left of the road to Snow Flat. The one-mile dirt road to Snow Flat is narrow, but not steep, and leads to a grassy meadow and a small pond. Park anywhere and have lunch. The trail that follows the creekbed below the pond leads, in less than a mile, to a small waterfall and a panoramic view of the valley far below. There are no facilities at Snow Flat, but camping is permitted there.

A mile above Snow Flat cutoff, you will see a road on your right leading to Shannon Campground. Here you will find drinking water, restrooms, and wonderful hiking trails. If you are going to hike, remember that you are at 9,100 feet; go slowly and give yourself a chance to adjust to the high altitude.

From Shannon Campground, there is a dirt road that climbs steeply for two miles up to Heliograph Lookout. General Nelson Miles' troops sent reflector messages from this peak, 10,028 feet high in an 1886 signalling network.

Two miles beyond Shannon, the road cuts through a clearing with the Hospital Flat Campground on your left. The campground is designed mainly for tents. Water and restrooms are available. Hospital Flat was so named because soldiers stationed at Fort Grant during the 1870s used this mountain meadow as a summer hospital for the many men wounded fighting the Apaches. The fort was abandoned as a military post in 1905, and is now a state prison.

The paved road ends as you leave Hospital Flat and head for Columbine, a Forest Service visitors center six miles up the road, open daily from Memorial Day to Labor Day. If you want a break, watch for the sign just beyond Columbine that points to Public Corrals. Take a right and after a quarter mile you'll be in a clearing with corrals on one side and a trail to Ash Creek two miles down the trail, where there are native trout in the icy mountain stream.

Soldier Creek Campground, situated at 9,300 feet and one mile beyond Columbine, is the highest camping area on the mountain and one of the most attractive. There are 11 camping units, drinking water, and even flush toilets.

A drive of 4.5 miles beyond Soldier Creek takes you to the trout-stocked Riggs Lake (8,600 feet) where there are 24 campsites, restrooms, and drinking water. While there is seldom anything resembling congestion in the Pinalenos, Riggs is easily the most popular campground, because of the lake. Campsites are better suited for tents because easy trailer pullouts and level ground are hard to find.

Trash barrels at Riggs Flat and other campgrounds are bear-proof, and therein lies a message: The Pinalenos are reputed to have the largest concentration of black bears in the West (possibly as many as 175 bears). The size of the bear population and the richness of the vegetation may be due to the fact that Swift Trail is closed each year for about six months, usually November 15 to Memorial Day depending on weather.

The dirt road continues another two miles beyond Riggs Flat. If it is solitude and wild country you're seeking, go beyond Riggs. There is a new pullout with restrooms on the right about half a mile beyond the Riggs cut-off. As human population dwindles, the wildlife population increases. You may see anything from a wild turkey to a peregrine falcon or a bear; undoubtedly, you will see a dozen shades of green in a lush forest of quaking aspen.

The only road back to Safford is the one you came in on, but take advantage of the return trip to see what you might have missed on the way to this mountain paradise.

— *Sam Negri*

(ABOVE) *Scenic overlooks along the Swift Trail will take your breath away. It was from such heights as this that the Army flashed its heliograph messages during the Apache campaign in 1886.*

(RIGHT) *Golden grasses carpet the shore and campground of Riggs Lake, elevation 8,600 feet. Campers should bring extra blankets. At this altitude warm days become chilly evenings.*

PHOTOS BY DAVID ELMS

Organ Pipe Cactus Landscape

A monument set aside for cactus brings to mind dry desert wastes barren of most life. But Organ Pipe Cactus National Monument in the southwestern corner of Arizona virtually overflows with beauty, a wide variety of Sonoran Desert flora and fauna, and two spectacular backroads guaranteed to make a desert lover out of almost anyone.

Spring, when the desert is awash with wildflowers and cactus blooms, is the best season to visit Organ Pipe, but a drive through the monument during any cooler season will enchant the back road enthusiast.

This is the Sonoran Desert at its best, an arid landscape of cactus and creosote bush interspersed with thickets of mesquite, ironwood, and paloverde trees. The intriguing, almost mysterious, terrain varies from rolling hills to deep arroyos and sandy washes to jutting volcanic peaks. The wildlife ranges from the lowly lizard and rattlesnake to the lithe pronghorn antelope and comical javelina (collared peccary).

When Spanish explorers first traversed this land it was inhabited by members of a peaceful, friendly race which had adapted to the desert environment and thrived in this arid land. They have been known as the Papagos (Spanish for "bean eaters") until recently when they legally changed their name to what they called themselves all along, Tohono O'odham, "the desert people."

Their reservation lies to the east of the monument, and you will drive across it if you come to Organ

Pipe from Tucson. If you have time, stop at any of the reservation villages and take a look at the exquisite Tohono O'odham basketry.

The Tohono O'odham still gather some of their food from the desert of the monument, and the proclamation President Franklin D. Roosevelt signed in 1937 creating the monument expressly protects

Best time to go	October through April
Degree of difficulty	Easy
Type of vehicle	Family car
Travel time	Ten hours; good overnight camping
Road type	Paved, gravel
Elevation	2,000 - 3,000 feet
Terrain	Desert
Features	Exceptional cacti, desert scenery

(ABOVE) *Myriad spring wildflowers at Organ Pipe Cactus National Monument.* JERRY SIEVE

(LEFT) *Saguaro sentinels guard the silent desert at sundown on the road to Organ Pipe Cactus National Monument. This journey to the Mexican border country of southwestern Arizona is most pleasant from fall through spring.* DAVID ELMS

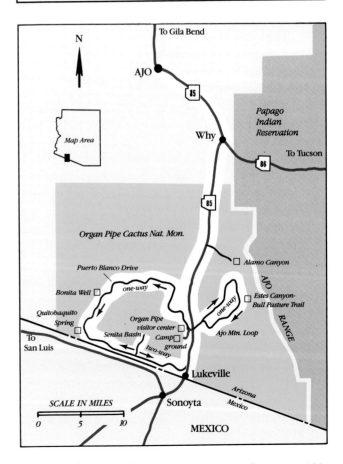

"the rights of the Indians of the Papago reservation to pick the fruits of the organ pipe cactus and other cactus . . . ."

The drive to Organ Pipe Cactus National Monument is roughly the same distance whether you travel from Phoenix or Tucson — about 130 miles. The former mining community of Ajo, on State Route 85 a dozen or so miles north of the monument boundary, has lodging, restaurants, medical facilities, and grocery stores. It is a good jumping off place for our tour. From Ajo, drive southeast on 85 to the junction with State Route 86 and the town of Why.

Many people have asked why Why is named Why. One philosopher once responded, "Why not?" The truth is that before the road was redesigned, it formed a "Y" where the settlement is located. Now it looks more like a "T".

Turn south at the "T" in Why and you will come, after 28 miles, to the visitor center at Organ Pipe Cactus National Monument. There is a $3 entrance fee, and an additional $8 per-night charge for camping. The campground, 1.5 miles from the visitor center, has 208 camping units. Drinking water and restrooms are available, but there are no electrical hookups

The park was named for a unique cactus, found only in this area, that looks like a pipe organ without a keyboard. The organ pipe cactus vaguely resembles the saguaro, but rather than having one main trunk with smaller branches, it has many branches which rise from a base in a cluster of thick arms that may grow as high as 20 feet. Like the saguaro, the organ pipe produces a huge blossom in May and June.

(ABOVE) *It's easy to see how the organ pipe cactus got its name. Unique to this area, these cacti may reach 20 feet in height and produce gorgeous blooms in late spring. Background is part of the 208-site main campground, about a mile from the visitor center at Organ Pipe Cactus National Monument.* JERRY SIEVE

OPPOSITE, CLOCKWISE FROM TOP
The Sonoran Desert viewed through a mountain arch along the 53-mile Puerto Blanco loop drive, is both vast and beautiful. DAVID ELMS

Quitobaquito Spring, one of the few oases in this arid land, has slaked the thirst of ancient Indians, Spanish conquistadors, and gold-seeking '49ers.
WESLEY HOLDEN

You will find this weathered corral at Bonita Well. It was part of a working cattle ranch before the area became a national monument in 1937. DAVID ELMS

Desert flora and distant mountains are always in sight. This scene was photographed on a March afternoon along the road to Senita Basin. DAVID ELMS

The Ajo Mountains
on the eastern margin
of Organ Pipe Cactus
National Monument
form a rugged backdrop
for saguaros and their
floral neighbors.
The 21-mile long
Ajo Mountain loop
is one of two popular
drives in the monument.
LARRY ULRICH

The senita cactus is another unusual plant that flourishes in the monument. It looks like a diminutive organ pipe, but the tips of each arm are covered with spiny whiskers which give it the name "senita" — Spanish for "old one."

Most travelers visit during the pleasant weather period between October and April, because summer temperatures often reach more than 100 degrees.

There are two scenic drives in the monument, which covers 516 square miles of rugged desert bordered by jagged mountain peaks. Both loops are graded gravel roads, easily maneuvered in a standard passenger vehicle, and both are beautiful.

To the west of the visitors center on State Route 85 is the 51-mile Puerto Blanco loop drive which leads, after 35 miles, to Quitobaquito Spring, a freshwater oasis in the middle of a bone-dry desert. In terms of natural phenomena, it is possibly as remarkable as the Grand Canyon, yet it did nothing for the imagination of one William T. Hornaday, a New York botanist who camped there during a 1907 expedition. In his memoir, *Campfires on Desert and Lava* he wrote, "Although Quitovaquita (sic) was entirely quiet and inoffensive, its atmosphere was depressing. It is one of the spots in which I would not like to die and would hate to live."

Like any reliable watering hole in Arizona, Quitobaquito has a long history. Melchior Diaz, a member of the Coronado expedition in 1540, probably stopped there. Jesuit missionary Eusebio Kino baptized Indian children near there in 1690 and described it simply as "a good place."

A man named Andrew Dorsey settled there in 1860 and dug the pond that is there today.

The other principal drive is the 21-mile Ajo Mountain loop which begins across State Route 85 from the visitors center and winds northeast to the jagged walls of the magenta-colored Ajo Mountains. There are two picnic areas along the route, one about five miles in and the other near the start of the Estes Canyon-Bull Pasture Trail.

The trail through Bull Pasture is 3.4 miles round-trip and passes through an area rich in wildlife and vegetation. It becomes steep as it nears the top of the canyon. As it turns sharply to the north, watch the walls alongside the trail for a large outcropping of obsidian, the shiny black mineral that Native Americans have used as material for tools and sculpture over the centuries.

On either drive in Organ Pipe Cactus National Monument the bird life is abundant, but especially at Quitobaquito Spring. Some 260 species have been sighted there. Cactus wrens, American kestrels, roadrunners, Gambel's quail, phainopeplas, curve-billed thrashers, turkey vultures, and red-tailed hawks are common. Golden eagles and prairie falcons also have been sighted.

The only road back to Ajo is the one which brought you to Organ Pipe Cactus National Monument. This is a wild, lonely, beautiful corner of our state, but it is well worth the effort to visit.

— *Sam Negri*

(ABOVE)
The Estes Canyon-Bull Pasture Trail is a favorite of hikers. There's no better way to see Sonoran Desert wildlife and vegetation up close.
GEORGE WUERTHNER

(OPPOSITE)
Purple owl clover and yellow brittlebush can usually be found in profusion along the Ajo Mountain drive from March through April.
JERRY SIEVE

DAVID ELMS

Historic Arivaca Country

Heintzelman Mine • Eighteenth century ranches
Quaint Arivaca • Ruby mining camp • Peña Blanca Lake

In rapidly-growing Tucson, you never have to go far to sample the rough-and-tumble life of a century and more ago. The Arivaca loop is a case in point. From metropolitan Tucson, it quickly takes you to a landscape where horses, cattle, and cowboys are still the dominant life forms. While the area looks primitive and remote, its isolation is mostly illusion: Never are you more than 20 miles from human habitation.

Begin the 145-mile loop drive by taking Interstate 19 south from Tucson 34 miles to Arivaca Junction (Exit 48). From the freeway off-ramp turn right, then right again at the access road. Driving north, you immediately enter Arivaca Junction. Take the first left, Arivaca Road, which curves past ranches and mesquite trees on its way to one of Arizona's oldest communities.

After 14.8 miles on Arivaca Road, an easily-missed dirt road to the right leads in .2 mile to an unmarked grave on the left, believed by some to be that of John Poston, murdered in 1861. The

(ABOVE) *A cow skull storefront creates an unforgettable image of the ranching country of southern Arizona at the Amado exit on Interstate 19.*

(LEFT) *Ranching, mining, unspoiled scenery, and two centuries of Arizona history make this drive a memorable experience. Mountains dwarf a cowboy and his horse on the road between Arivaca and Ruby.*
PHOTOS BY J. PETER MORTIMER

buff-colored Cerro Colorado range rises in the distance. Among those hills, the Heintzelman Mine (also called the Cerro Colorado) opened in 1856. Promoted as one of the world's richest silver mines, it attracted heavy investment from famous gun inventor Samuel Colt.

Arivaca is 23 miles west of Arivaca Junction, 8.4 miles beyond the gravesite turn-off. Just before the outskirts of town, the Buenos Aires National Wildlife Refuge has set up Arivaca Cienega Trail, a lush nature trail that is handicapped accessible

Best time to go	All year
Degree of difficulty	Easy to moderate
Type of vehicle	High clearance preferred; sedan can make it
Travel time	Six hours
Road type	Paved, dirt
Elevation	3,000 - 4,000 feet
Terrain	Grassland, foothills
Features	Historic towns, canyon hikes, lakes

and offers great bird-watching. The U.S. Fish and Wildlife Service provides birding lists at its information office in Arivaca (next to the well-stocked Arivaca Mercantile Company).

Arivaca has a population of about 150 in the town proper. Besides the general store (with its gas pump), "downtown" Arivaca includes a restaurant, feed and hardware store, public library, and artists co-op. Turn right on Fourth Avenue to see the town's historic schoolhouse and cemetery.

Arivaca was occupied long before Heintzelman's miners arrived. Like much of southern Arizona, it was first populated by Pima and Tohono O'odham (formerly Papago) Indians. In the 1700s, Spaniards came because of its abundant water and grazing and mining potential. Known then as a ranch called "La Aribac," it was abandoned after an Indian uprising in 1751. In 1812, four decades before the Gadsden Purchase made the area part of the United States, Augustin Ortiz bought the ranch from the Spanish colonial government. Heintzelman's mining company purchased all of Ortiz's rights in 1856.

Where Arivaca Road forms a "T" with Fifth Avenue, turn left, heading roughly east on Ruby Road. The road is paved to the county line.

Arivaca Lake turnoff is five miles beyond the townsite, going 2.3 miles off Ruby Road. The lake is presently contaminated with mercury (possibly from old mines in the watershed), so all warm-water fishing is catch and release only. Call the Arizona Game and Fish office in Tucson, (520) 628-5376, for a recorded fishing update.

Not far beyond the lake turnoff, the pavement ends and the road becomes a true back road — winding and narrow, with washboard ruts, sizable rocks, and switchbacks. A sedan can make it, but not low-clearance or wide-body vehicles like motor

(OPPOSITE, TOP TO BOTTOM) *Delightfully deserted, this back road leads south from Arivaca, the peaceful community of about 150 folks who shun the city life. The Tohono O'odham Indians thrived here more than 200 years ago when the Spanish explored the area and mined silver from the surrounding mountains.*

Not far from the Heintzelman Mine and only 200 yards north of the Arivaca road is the grave of John Poston, brother of Charles Poston, "father of Arizona." John Poston was murdered in 1861 by the mine laborers who stole more than $70,000 in bullion.

Arivaca ranch country, a land of rugged mountains and high desert vegetation.

Arivaca's small business district provides the essentials for most residents and visitors.

(ABOVE) *South of Arivaca lies the town of Ruby, named for the postmaster's wife in 1902.*

(RIGHT) *A quintessential Arizona sunset bleeds across the sky between Ruby and Peña Blanca Lake.*
PHOTOS BY J. PETER MORTIMER

(ABOVE) *One of southern Arizona's most beautiful areas is Sycamore Canyon, a few miles southeast of Ruby. Hiking, camping and bird watching are popular here.*

(LEFT) *Every turn in the road brings interesting scenery, such as this view between Hank and Yank Spring and Peña Blanca Lake.*

(ABOVE RIGHT) *Fishermen land bass, bluegill, catfish, and trout at Peña Blanca Lake, 17 miles northwest of Nogales.*

(INSET) *One of southern Arizona's favorite recreational resources, Peña Blanca Lake is a fitting finale for this backroad adventure.*

PHOTOS BY J. PETER MORTIMER

homes. Top speed is no more than 20 miles per hour. Road conditions vary seasonally, and if it's raining, don't go.

The drive from here to Peña Blanca Lake takes several hours, but the scenery is ruggedly beautiful. Deer and colorful birds can be spotted, even in mid-day.

Just 6.6 miles past the Arivaca Lake turnoff is Ruby, a gold mining camp founded as the Montana Mine in the 1890s. Postmaster Julius Andrews named the town for his wife, Lillie Ruby, in 1902. Privately owned, Ruby is one of Arizona's best-preserved ghost towns. At this time, the owners allow hiking, picnicking, and bass fishing, if you first buy a permit. Call (520) 744-4471 or write Ruby Mines, 6202 West Ina Road, Tucson, Arizona 85743. Group rates are available.

Five miles beyond Ruby, the road again comes to a "T." Turn right. After driving .1 mile, you'll see the sign for Sycamore Canyon. A right turn and another 100 yards south takes you to the trailhead of this uncongested hiking and picnicking spot.

Down the trail is the sign for "Hank and Yank Spring," named for 1880s ranchers Hank Hewitt and "Yank" Bartlett. Almost immediately, the trail enters the tree-lined creekbed and the Goodding Research Natural Area (camping discouraged here). Botanist Leslie Goodding discovered rare local plants in the early 1900s. The canyon, filled with boulders, caves, and oak and sycamore trees, is surrounded by the Pajarito and Atascosa mountains.

About eight miles past the Sycamore Canyon turnoff, you return to pavement. You're now on State Route 289. Take the highway left past the campgrounds, and it dead-ends at Peña Blanca Lake. Camping, picnicking, hiking, and boating are available, but all other facilities are temporarily closed at this time. Warm-water fishing is catch and release only since Peña Blanca also is contaminated with mercury, likely from an old mining mill site upstream.

It is 9.3 miles on pavement from the lake to Interstate 19. Drive south 7.5 miles to Nogales or return 57 miles north to Tucson. — *Sam Negri*

Tour 19: 60 Miles, Starts from Nogales

Scenic Mexican Border

San Rafael Valley • Mowry's mine • Ghost towns
Parker Canyon • Coronado National Memorial

Along the rolling, grass-carpeted hills of the San Rafael Valley, cattle graze peacefully. Cow punchers have been working these ranges for some 200 years. Thick groves of oak trees dot the foothills, and a stately old house sits atop a hill overlooking the former border station of Lochiel.

On the eastern slopes of the Patagonia Mountains lie crumbling adobe ruins and rusting mining equipment, the last vestiges of those boisterous boomtowns of yesteryear. They all invite the adventurer to explore this colorful land along one of Arizona's most historic and picturesque back roads.

If you're traveling along Interstate 19 south of Tucson, a good warmup for this scenic 60-mile journey along the Mexican border is a visit to the old Spanish missions of San Xavier and Tumacacori, followed by a shopping trip to Nogales. You may want to spend the night in that border city. Then you'll have a fresh start in the morning and

a chance to spend the entire day exploring and taking short trips off the main route.

Traveling northeast out of Nogales on State Route 82, the Patagonia-Sonoita Scenic Road, turn right at Kino Springs Country Club, four miles east of Nogales, and follow the main road through the club, crossing the bridge over the Santa Cruz River. Some five miles east of the country club is the settlement of Kino Springs. Take the dirt road east toward the Patagonia Mountains. From this point, you'll be driving along unpaved but generally well-maintained roads. Except where mentioned, all are easily traveled by automobile, but during heavy rains, don't go — even by four-wheel-drive vehicle.

Plan to stop at the crest of the Patagonias and have a look around. The scenery is simply spectacular. Off to the east lie the San Rafael Valley and the headwaters of the Santa Cruz River. The wandering little river meanders to the

(ABOVE) *This monument near Lochiel in the San Rafael Valley marks the spot where many people believe Fray Marcos de Niza entered Arizona in 1530.* DON B. STEVENSON

(OPPOSITE) *The San Rafael Ranch in the cattle country of southeastern Arizona near Lochiel.* JACK DYKINGA

Best time to go
All year

Degree of difficulty
Easy to moderate

Type of vehicle
Family car

Travel time
Six hours, good overnight camping

Road type
Dirt, rough in spots

Elevation
3,500 - 6,000 feet

Terrain
Mountains, forest

Features
Scenic vistas, history

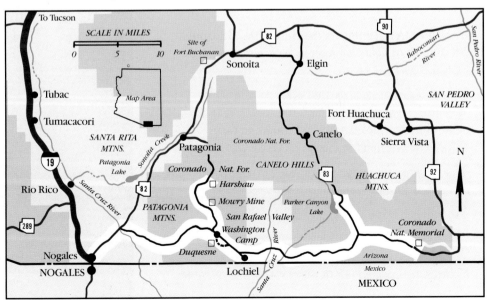

south past Lochiel into Mexico, then curves around in a northwesterly direction and re-enters Arizona just east of Nogales on the old Buenavista Ranch.

Looking back toward Nogales, you'll get a panoramic vista of rugged mountains that mark the Santa Cruz watershed.

Traveling down the eastern slope of the Patagonias, you'll see an old gravity-fed ore chute resting beside the road — mute testimony to the bygone days when silver was king. In 1860 a flamboyant ex-Army officer named Sylvester Mowry acquired title to a rich silver mine near here. The ore was amenable to direct smelting, saving the expense of transporting it. Mowry poured his own bullion and became prosperous. He enjoyed a colorful career as a politician, entrepreneur, and a leader in the struggle to create the Territory of Arizona.

Journalists who passed through these mountains around 1860 were awestruck by the pristine beauty of the land and the richness of its mines. However, marauding Apaches were a constant threat, especially to travelers along these lonely trails. In 1857, at nearby Sonoita Creek, the Army established Fort Buchanan to protect the miners and settlers. When the Civil War began in 1861 the post was abandoned. Chiricahua Apaches under Cochise went on the warpath and for several years this part of Arizona was a "dark and bloody ground."

Part way down the slope you'll come to a junction. The road to the right, Forest Road 61, goes to Washington Camp and Lochiel.

On the left fork, if you want to take a brief side trip, are the ghost towns of Mowry and Harshaw, the former is the site of Sylvester Mowry's silver mine.

(PANORAMA) *Evening on the crest of the Patagonia Mountains as lights blink on in Nogales, to the west.* DON B. STEVENSON

(INSETS, COUNTER-CLOCKWISE FROM TOP LEFT) *A century ago, ore from Duquesne, and a half dozen other mines, rumbled down the chutes and was reduced at Washington Camp.* GEORGE WUERTHNER

This old house is about all that's left at Duquesne, once a booming mining camp.

Abandoned mine shafts, such as this one at the Mowry Mine, are treacherous.

A high fence marks the Mexican boundary at picturesque Lochiel. PHOTOS BY DON B. STEVENSON

Half a dozen crumbling adobe walls and some rusted remnants of bygone days still remain of Mowry, now posted as private property and barely visible north of Forest Road 134 near the junction with Forest Road 49. Harshaw was once a bustling town of 2,000. A hillside cemetery, a couple of wood shanties, and a brick building are all that's left.

Washington Camp is another once-thriving mining town. For another brief side trip, go south of Washington Camp on Forest Road 128, a rough-rutted road that twists and turns up a hill a mile to Duquesne, where silver and copper mining provided a profit of $185,000 for the mine owner by 1917. (Don't drive your passenger car on this road.)

Heading south from Duquesne, rejoin Forest Road 61 for a four-mile journey to Lochiel. Flora in this area includes manzanita, cedar, scrub oak, Mexican piñon pine, ponderosa, gray-green needled Chihuahua pine, Apache pine, and Arizona sycamore.

Off to the east is the rolling, grass-covered San Rafael Valley. There are several ranches in the valley, but the most famous is the venerable San Rafael Cattle Company, once a Mexican land grant dating back to the 1820s. Later it was owned by Colonel William C. Greene, the mining entrepreneur and Wall Street giant. His descendants still own the ranch.

If this part of the country looks like something out of a western movie — well, in fact, it is. Such westerns as *Monte Walsh* and *Tom Horn* were filmed nearby. Back in the 1950s, *Oklahoma!* was filmed right here. Searching for the unspoiled paradise that was Oklahoma Territory at the turn of the century, the film crew chose Arizona. The abundant Oklahoma crops used in the movie don't thrive here, so wax substitutes were used. They had to be replaced regularly because the "fruit" melted in the Arizona sun.

Lochiel now basks quietly in the shade of tall trees. It is believed that Fray Marcos de Niza passed through here in April, 1539 on his reconnaissance mission for the Coronado expedition. A monument alongside the road commemorates that event.

Our destination, heading east on Forest Road 61, is the Coronado National Memorial, 28 miles down the dirt road on the south end of the Huachuca Mountains. You are now traveling just a short distance north of the Mexican border, in some of the best ranch and game country in Arizona. If you're watchful or lucky, you might see antelope, javelina, wild turkey, Mearns' quail, ducks in migration, or whitetail and mule deer.

(TOP LEFT) *Parker Canyon Lake, only 11 miles from Lochiel, is one of southern Arizona's better fishing lakes.*

(INSET LEFT) *A great place to bring the kids to experience nature, and have family fun.*

(ABOVE) *The trail from the memorial and picnic area to Coronado Peak is about .5 mile. It provides views of Mexico and the San Pedro and San Rafael valleys.*

(RIGHT) *The ramada at the end of the Coronado Peak Trail burned in a 1988 forest fire, but was replaced. The rest of the trail suffered no damage.*

(BELOW RIGHT) *In this late afternoon view, Looking west from the memorial, you can see the road you just traveled.*
PHOTOS BY DON B. STEVENSON

By watching the signs, you can take a side trip to Parker Canyon Lake, where the fishing is good. Farther up the Parker Canyon road is Canelo, where the Arizona Nature Conservancy has a preserve. This is Arizona wine country, and a short distance from Elgin is a winery where visitors are welcome.

On the main trail you are going to make a steep climb up to a saddle in the Huachuca Mountains, to the memorial honoring the Coronado expedition of 1540-42. Here you can enjoy a sweeping view of the high plains of Mexico, the San Pedro Valley, and all the brawny mountain islands that dot this vast area.

Being able to look back at where you've driven from such a lofty vantage point seems a fitting way to end your back road *jornada* along the scenic Mexican border. — *Marshall Trimble*

Chiricahua Adventure

Portal • Rustler Park • Chiricahua National Monument
Rare birds • Mountain scenery

Once the homeland of Apache leader Cochise, and later the province of desperado cowboys, homesteaders, and miners, the Chiricahua Mountains are now regarded as one of the most picturesque outdoor recreation areas in the state of Arizona. Almost the entire range is federally protected, either as part of the Coronado National Forest or as the Chiricahua National Monument.

The range situated in the southeastern corner of Arizona is about 20 miles wide and 40 miles long. On the drive over the top of the mountain you will pass through five biological life zones, from cactus to spruce and aspen forests.

It was at Rustler Park, the campground at the top of the range, where outlaws hid their stolen livestock in territorial times. Nowadays, the meadow at Rustler Park, filled with wild irises in late spring, is a favorite destination for campers, hikers, birdwatchers, and backpackers preparing to enter the Chiricahua Wilderness area.

Easily the best way to see the range — best because it is the most scenic and offers the most options — is to drive a loop that begins in the ranching community of Willcox, heads east to San Simon, south to Paradise and Portal; and then goes over the top of the range, drops down to the Sulphur Springs Valley, and returns to Willcox.

From Tucson, take Interstate 10 east to the Rex Allen Drive exit at Willcox, a distance of 89 miles. All tourist facilities, including supermarkets and medical services, are available at Willcox. Continue

(ABOVE LEFT) *The thick-billed parrot is a colorful native reintroduced to the Cave Creek area near the Southwest Research Station.* GEORGE H. H. HUEY

(OPPOSITE) *You can view the erosion-sculpted forms of the Wonderland of Rocks in Chiricahua National Monument from the scenic drive, but to explore the most spectacular region, Heart of Rocks, requires a nine-mile hike.* DON B. STEVENSON

Best time to go
March to November

Degree of difficulty
Easy to moderate

Type of vehicle
High clearance preferred;
sedan can make it

Travel time
Eight hours, good
overnight camping

Road type
Dirt, rocky in spots

Elevation
3,500 - 7,000 feet

Terrain
Mountains, desert

Features
Scenery, history
exceptional birdwatching

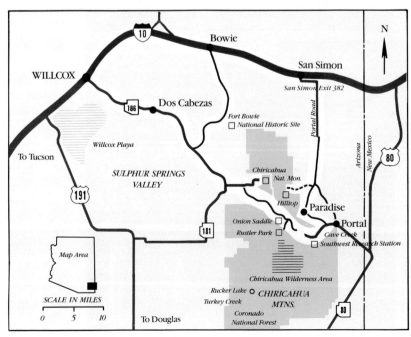

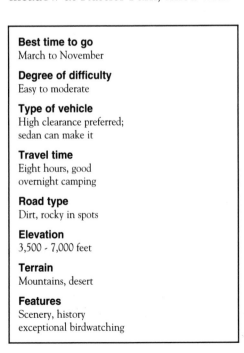

east 44 miles on Interstate 10 to exit 382, the second San Simon exit (Portal Road). It loops around and parallels Interstate 10 for .75 mile before the Portal Road shoots off to the right (south). The road is paved for the next nine miles, but then it becomes dirt.

Nineteen miles south of Interstate 10 you will come to a junction marked with signs. The road to the right leads into Whitetail Canyon, a three mile side trip which takes you to the long-abandoned Hilltop Mine. If you don't take the Whitetail side trip you have two options: The road on the left goes directly to Portal; the middle road, leading to Portal via the tiny community of Paradise, is the more scenic but it is suitable only for high clearance vehicles.

Paradise, 25 miles south of I-10, was once a swinging spot. Outlaws from Tombstone used to make their headquarters in the early 1880s at nearby Galeyville, now vanished from the map. Take a left at the mailboxes in Paradise; the road winds six miles into the sleepy hamlet of Portal at the base of the dramatic rhyolite cliffs of Cave Creek Canyon. Do not follow the road directly into Paradise. Although you will see a sign that tells you Rustler Park is only 11 miles in that direction, this road bypasses Portal and is very rough. Take that left at the mailboxes, go to Portal, and then to Rustler Park.

At Portal there is a tiny grocery store and restaurant, bed and breakfast, a motel and several campgrounds. The nearest gas station is in Rodeo, New Mexico, 10 miles to the east. Portal is home to the Southwest Research Station of the American Museum of Natural History.

(OPPOSITE, TOP) *Yuccas bloom in late spring along the road to Paradise.* WESLEY HOLDEN

(CENTER) *You're really on a back road here, and it narrows even more approaching Paradise.*

(BOTTOM) *The post office at Portal, only six miles from the New Mexico line, serves a lot of territory.*

(RIGHT) *Turkey Creek, high in the Chiricahuas, cascades down the mountain.* PHOTOS BY DON B. STEVENSON

(LOWER RIGHT) *Fall finery, particularly in the abundant maple trees, makes Cave Creek a riot of color.*

(BELOW) *It is characteristic of Cave Creek's volcanic walls to be riddled with stony, cave-like alcoves.* PHOTOS BY PETER KRESNAN

(BOTTOM) *Rucker Lake, 10 miles south of Rustler Park, bears the name of Lieutenant John A. Rucker, who gave his life trying to save a fellow officer from drowning in the flooding creek which fills this scenic lake.* DON B. STEVENSON

Scientists come from all over the world to do ecological research here. The facility houses a collection of local flora and fauna, including 244 species of birds and 74 of mammals. A former director has noted that more such research is conducted in the Chiricahua Mountains than in any other field area in the nation.

The South Fork of Cave Creek Canyon, on the left before you reach the research station, is home to one of the richest lodes of birdlife in the United States. Many years ago it was found to be the northernmost range of a colorful parrot-like bird called the elegant trogon, and ever since then the world has been literally beating a path to the trogons' doorstep.

There is only one road over the Chiricahuas. It leads from the Portal store and past the research station before it begins to switchback up to Onion Saddle, 16 miles from Portal. Trailers longer than 16 feet are not permitted on this road, which can be bumpy at times. On most curves, there is barely room for two cars to pass safely, so be careful.

At Onion Saddle, go left two miles to Rustler Park Campground. Summertime temperatures here are typically in the 70s during the day and the 40s at night. Outhouses and drinking water are available.

Rustler Park is the gateway to the Chiricahua Wilderness area. The Crest Trail that leads out of Rustler Park wanders among pines, aspens, and spruce that are separated by flower-filled meadows called "parks." Long Park, Fly Park, Round Park, Anita Park, Junction Saddle, and Monte Vista Lookout (a fire watchtower) are points you can reach on Crest Trail.

To head back to Willcox from Rustler Park and complete the loop, return to Onion Saddle and turn left (west). Twelve miles down the mountain the pavement begins again. Take a right at this point and visit the Chiricahua National Monument, one of Arizona's great scenic showplaces. Here you'll find a visitors center with interpretive materials, a campground, numerous hiking trails, and a wonderland of fantastically shaped rocks teetering on surrounding cliffs. They seem to have their own personalities: Duck on a Rock, Mushroom Rock, and Punch and Judy, among others.

On the road back to Willcox, the travail that dominated this landscape during the Indian wars can be felt powerfully at Fort Bowie National Historic Site. From its founding in 1862 until the surrender of Geronimo in 1886, this fort was the center of military operations against the Chiricahua Apaches.

It is four miles from Chiricahua National Monument to the junction of State Route 186, and nine miles from there to the cutoff to Fort Bowie. There is a one-mile foot path to the fort which passes a reconstructed Apache village and the remnants of a Butterfield Overland Stage Station before you reach the adobe remains of the fort.

From the Fort Bowie turnoff, head west again on Highway 186. The road will curve through the historic ghost town of Dos Cabezas, which is still inhabited by a handful of families, and then turn slightly north to Willcox.
— *Sam Negri*

(OPPOSITE, TOP) *Stop by the visitors center at Chiricahua National Monument for information on the area, and great hiking trails.* DON B. STEVENSON

(CENTER) *Historic Dos Cabezas. In the 1870's mining caused the town to flourish.* WESLEY HOLDEN

(BOTTOM) *View from Heart of Rocks towards the Dos Cabezas Mountains.* PETER KRESNAN

(ABOVE LEFT) *The Balanced Rocks along Bonita Canyon Road are typical of the geologic oddities in the amazing Chiricahuas.* PETER KRESNAN

(INSET) *A Magnificent hummingbird sips from a coral bean in the bird-rich Chiricahuas.* G.C. KELLY

(LEFT) *Fort Bowie is a ruin now, but it guarded travelers on the road through Apache Pass. After Geronimo's group was captured and removed from Arizona the importance of the fort declined. It was abandoned in 1894.* JACK DYKINGA

Travel Tips

Detailed Forest Service recreation maps

can add much to your enjoyment. Several trips in this book are in or near Arizona's seven national forests. These maps cost $1 each at most ranger stations and forest headquarters. Tonto National Forest, 2324 East McDowell Road, Phoenix, has maps for all Arizona forests. These and other detailed Arizona maps of selected areas are available at map stores and some sporting goods stores.

When you meet another vehicle

on a narrow, unpaved road, look for an opportunity to pull to the right and let the other party pass. Most people will do the same for you. The courtesy is acknowledged by a wave or a nod.

Watch your gas gauge,

and fill up before you leave a populated area. Steep grades and rough roads can use up a lot of gas, and in Arizona it can sometimes be a l-o-n-g way between towns. Make sure your spare tire is properly inflated; many travelers overlook this.

Always carry a gallon or more of water,

and consider carrying snacks or a picnic lunch. It's a long way between cafes on some trips.

Forests and brushlands

can become explosively dry. Be careful with fire.

Be wary of stopping on the roadway,

even when the view is breathtaking or a flock of wild turkeys crosses the road. Pull well off the road, because not everyone travels Arizona's back roads at a prudent speed.

State and federal laws prohibit

damaging, defacing, or removing natural features—rocks, plants, trees, etc. And law enforcement is especially strict regarding vandalism or theft from Indian ruins.

Leave signs, gates

and other structures, the way you find them. Not much is "abandoned," and even structures that seem derelict belong to someone.

With dependable modern vehicles,

you should not have any emergency situations. But just in case, let someone know where you are going, and when they should hear from you again.

Carry your trash with you

until you find a proper container. There are usually garbage cans at roadside rest areas, U.S. Forest Service and National Park Service sites, state parks, and in front of many commercial establishments. Littering is punishable by a fine of up to $500. So stash that trash.

PETER ENSENBERGER

Index

Pages that are in **Boldface** denote photos. Pages followed by an "m" denote map.

Index